THE
BIG FISH

THE

BIG FISH

Edited by Arthur Oglesby
and Lucy Money-Coutts

ROBINSON
London

First published by
Robinson Publishing
11 Shepherd House
Shepherd Street
London W1Y 7LD

ISBN 1 85487 137 4

Typeset by Hewer Text Composition Services, Edinburgh

Printed and bound by Mackays of Chatham, Kent

10 9 8 7 6 5 4 3 2 1

CONTENTS

LIST OF ILLUSTRATIONS

1. Georgina Ballantine and her record salmon.
2. Major A. W. Huntington with 50-pounder.
3. Harold de Pass, one of the Awe big fish club.
4. Mr Thornton's 'portmanteau', 56lb.
5. Anthony Crossley and some of his catches.
6. 'Tiny' Morison with her 61lb Deveron Salmon.
7. The 'Uske' salmon, 1782.
8. A page from Miss Ballantine's scrapbook.
9. Edward Cochrane with the record Loch Lomond salmon.
10. D. C. Dinesen with his Jutland 58lb salmon.
11. Martin Skorve with J. R. Holden's 59lb Evanger salmon.
12. A. B. Ashby's 58-pounder.
13. Arthur Oglesby with his first big salmon from Norway. (*Arthur Oglesby*)
14. Terry Golding and a 49$^{1}/_{2}$lb salmon from the Vosso.
15. A 50-pounder from the Alta. (*Arthur Oglesby*)
16. Rupert Ponsonby with 14lb South Uist sea trout.
17. Michael Smith, aged eight, with 34lb Tay salmon.
18. Odd Haraldsen heading upstream on the Alta.
19. Georg Stromme of Voss, Norway, with his day's catch from the Vosso, June 1954.
20. 2176lb shark from Hermanus, South Africa.
21. A surprise sturgeon.
22. Lilla Rowcliffe with her 45lb salmon from the Spey.
23. Alison Faulkner with her 22lb Falkland sea trout.
24. A 19lb brown trout from Loch Arkaig, 1972.

INTRODUCTION

by Arthur Oglesby

I was first introduced to angling as a callow youth back in the 1930s. It was to be a highly traumatic experience which imbued me with a life-long love of the outdoors and so many aspects of natural history. There was something magical about the study and capture of creatures outside the natural environment of *homo sapiens*. So, to my youthful mind, every piece of water, whether a small village pond or a massive Scottish loch, was held to contain leviathans of a size quite beyond my juvenile comprehension.

After the Second World War I again took up fishing with renewed interest. But now I had set my sights firmly on game fish and so there began a long and demanding apprenticeship in order that I might become as good an angler as lay within my capability.

A good angler, particularly a fly fisherman, not only has to be an above-average caster, but he also requires that keenly-developed stealth and cunning of the hunter. God had bestowed on me an adequate talent for hunting, but I had to work hard to acquire any dexterity with my tackle. It was to be an on-going process which would quickly make me realise that as an angler I could never become totally fulfilled and that it would need more than one lifetime to approach the threshold of full knowledge.

It was that great American fisherman Edward Hewitt who wrote of the three stages of the angler:

1

1. When he/she wants to catch the most fish
2. When he/she wants to catch the biggest fish
3. When he/she is only interested in the most difficult fish
    regardless of quantity or size.

The prospect of catching a larger than average fish, of whatever species, is always exciting. Nowadays some of our coarse fishermen form specimen-hunting groups and apply great dedication to the exploitation of all legitimate angling methods to catch a trophy fish.

In former times most big salmon and sea trout came from rivers with a big fish reputation. Such British waters which come to mind include the English Wye, Avon and Eden; the Welsh Dee and the Scottish Tay, Tweed, Dee and Awe. Occasional monsters could be coaxed from the Spey, Deveron or Nith, but it was only by making a pilgrimage across the North Sea to Norway that anglers could hope to encounter the real leviathans.

Thus it was the early British sportsmen who first discovered the tremendous angling potential of Norway. With a coastline covering over 2000 miles, the country offered some of the finest fishing for the bigger Atlantic salmon ever known. But, with few exceptions, the rivers of Norway rarely offered great numbers of fish, although there were several which could and did, produce their quota of very big ones.

The reputation for the biggest Norwegian salmon was held by the Tana river in northern Norway. Reports are unconfirmed about actual weights, but two fish of 76lb are recorded along with two of 74lb from the same river. Additionally, another six fish of over 70lb are listed from such rivers as the Aroy, Namsen, Vefsna and Passvik and there is a deluge of fish recorded in the 50lb to 70lb bracket. Around the turn of the century, fish of over 50lb were not considered exceptional in Norway and such rivers as the Alta, Vosso, Laerdal, Sundalslagen or Sand, Gaula, Orkla, Rauma, Mals, Drive and Jolstra, all produced specimens exceeding this weight.

One memorable catch from the Vosso of two fish weighing 64lb and 55lb was made on 30 June 1954 by Georg Stromme of Voss on the Liland beat. Another fish of 53lb, taken from the same river by a Danish angler, proved to be the first fish he had ever caught while fishing for the first time in his life.

Fifty-pounders were still commonplace during the period of my first serious visit to the Bolstad beat of the Vosso in June 1966. In the few weeks before my arrival no less than eight fish of over 50lb had been recorded and this included one of over 60lb. With hindsight, I suppose that I was instrumental in giving the Vosso a reputation it did not wholly deserve, but while it was not a prolific river, it continued to produce salmon of an average weight of 28lb for many years. Indeed, the late Cyril Mowbray Wells, who was a tenant of the Bolstad beat between the wars, took to his own rod, eighty salmon weighing over 40lb. Miraculously, his eightieth fish over that weight was taken on his eightieth birthday.

So where are the big fish in 1992? The Vosso has been so short of fish over the past few seasons that it has now been closed to all angling and estuary netting. The legendary Laerdal nearly suffered the same fate and many of the hitherto classical Norwegian rivers are but mere shadows of their former selves. Of course, the decline is not confined to big fish. Salmon catches generally, in Britain, Norway and North America are in serious decline and there is much keen speculation and research being undertaken by those who earnestly seek an answer to the problem.

If the big fish have almost gone, what might have caused their decline? One of my long-held theories (and I don't really like theories about fish and fishing, for history often proves them wrong) is that the more a species is exploited or threatened, the smaller the average size becomes. My four fish of over 40lb from the Vosso were regarded as commonplace when I caught them, but where could you go today with even a remote prospect of hooking a 40-pounder? For all my experience of British rivers, I have yet to catch a fish bigger than 27lb and the chances of my exceeding this fade with every passing year. The odds stacked against the salmon are too great. Not only do they suffer from over-exploitation by mankind, but they have to face untold hazards from acid rain, pollution, pesticides and fertilisers on the land, treated and untreated sewage and a total lack of meaningful river management.

But in offering our readers a bountiful measure of nostalgia, Lucy Money-Coutts and myself have had great joy in sifting through many tales of glorious battles with monstrous fish. Into Lucy's lap fell the daunting task of researching all the stories featured in the book, coupled with the sheer drudgery of locating reliable sources of material. It is our hope that you will enjoy these journeys into the past. But note the tinge of sadness. Might it be a history which is unlikely to be repeated?

NORWAY

A Great Fish from the Vosso

Reading the accounts in a recent book, *Salmon and Women*, of the three great salmon, all caught by women in U.K. by:

Miss Ballantine 64lb R. Tay, 7 October 1922. Spin. U.K.
Record Rod and Line
Mrs Morison 61lb R. Deveron, 21 October 1924. Fly. U.K.
Record Fly
Miss Davey 59½lb R. Wye, 13 March 1923. Spin. U.K.
Record Spring Fish

has made me consider rewriting my account of the great salmon I caught at Evanger on the Vosso on 23 June 1949, not to "cook the books", but before this I had only caught three or four small salmon in England and two of 27½lb and 29½lb at Evanger on 21 June 1949. I really had at that time little idea of what was actually going on down there under the water. Now, nearly 700 salmon later, I can make an informed guess.

The Vosso river, as big as or bigger than Tay or Tweed, rises in the mountains of S.W. Norway, passes through Voss, thence to Evanger which is immediately above the famous Bolstad beat which runs down into Bergen Fiord. The Bergen-Oslo railway runs up its East Bank from Bergen to Voss and beyond.

The salmon fishing starts in June as soon as the loose snow falling after Christmas has melted and run off. The packed snow falling before Christmas and the underlying glacier is still slowly melting and on a sunny day the river may rise four inches or more. It was always crystal clear and when we arrived I was told that it was running at about four feet above dead summer low.

The beat at Evanger has two great pools, Skorve at the lower end and Ho at the top, and a few lesser resting-places.

My tackle, a fairly heavy split cane spinning rod belonging to Biddy's father for fishing in Norway – its fault, no rock-firm "bedding" for the reel. A good orthodox spinning reel for those days, comfortably holding 200 yards of plaited nylon line, 15lb breaking strain. A five-inch golden sprat on a Dee tackle (celluloid casing and fins with two treble hooks in tandem) all of the highest possible quality. No economy between the reel and the sprat's tail. Lead weights adjusted by trial and error. Harling is backing down river by boat in figures of eight, spinning with 25 yards of line out from the stern of the boat. The skill is of course the boatman's. It is he who "presents" the lure to the salmon.

The keeper, Martin Skorve (same name as the pool and his farm) and I were fishing alone; the rest of our party had gone to see a film about the Norwegian Resistance and there is little doubt but that I ought to have gone, too – however . . . We started harling with a five-inch golden sprat on Dee tackle at about 9 p.m., more importantly, it was not until the sun had sunk well below the Western Mountains and the glare had gone off the water. It had been a bright and sunny day and the river was running clear. We had fished to well down Skorve Osen (Osen is the tail of a pool) without any incidents and had reached the stage when Martin said "Lit lange nie" and I let out five yards of line and then again "Lit lange nie" and out goes another five yards. The line is released more or less in one go and lets the sprat "free fall" downstream. This is always considered a likely taking-time. Take he did at about 9.40 p.m. with what I originally described as "two trout-like jags and then a heavy pull". This I now interpret as the fish going upstream as it took the sprat, then shaking its head twice against a relatively slack line, then turning to face downstream; this was the heavy pull and when I tightened on it.

I should say at this stage that the Skorve Osen ran out into an impassable rapid. All were agreed that going down it could in no circumstances be contemplated, unlike Ho Osen (the top pool) where the keeper could shoot the rapid if a good fish went down. (Twenty-five kroner to bring the boat back by horse and cart, I believe.)

A recognised tactic if a fish was thought to be going to run down out of a pool was to let out say 50 to 75 yards of line as fast as possible, the current turning this line into a great bulge below the fish which would think it was being pulled downstream from below and make off upstream as desired. I knew nothing of all this.

To return to the battle, the fish, seemingly well-hooked now, let itself be as it were "walked up" about 120 yards upstream by steady rowing. It then took off, facing downstream, about 150 yards in one great rush then turned to face upstream of its own accord. Only about 25 yards of line left on the reel at this stage, I could see the reel "spars". It was then "walked up" again under heavy pressure and much line recovered – I felt better. Martin said it was "Stor, stor lax," I think this was because of the very slow rhythm of its head-shaking. Then the worst time came. It backed downstream (facing upstream) in bursts of ten yards or so. Evidently, from the great pressure that it exerted, it was backing and letting the stream catch its enormous flank. By now it was nearly back to its starting point and then things started to go wrong.

The reel fitting slipped so that the reel was turned 90° to one side of the rod rings and the reel spun out of control. One of the reel handles caught my thumb which knocked the handle off. I heard Martin groan.

I think I must have unwittingly let out enough line to do the bulge trick referred to above. At any rate although the mean pressure seemed more and the line started to hum, the dreadful jagging bursts had stopped and it is now obvious to me that the salmon was making its way upstream against the pressure of current on a great bulge of drowned line behind it.

Boat and fish now moved about 70 yards upstream with a tremendous strain on the bulge. Then the fish wallowed for the first time, nearly level with the boat. The danger now was that it would soon lie on its side and flop downstream out of control – just a few minutes left to recover the bulge and tow it out of the current into the quieter water where Martin indicated that it *must not* regain the main stream. It only made two rather half-hearted attempts to do so. The tempo changed – we were in charge for the first time, thence to the landing stage, too far for it to reach the current now. At the landing stage there was a nice very slow current, just enough to keep the fish's head upstream and plenty of depth. The great fight in the current had tired it out and about five minutes from leaving the current we were into the end game. How awful to lose it now!

I got out of the boat and climbed up a steep grassy bank, slipped and fell twice on this but having gained the top, I could see for the first time the fish's enormous size, though it was still pretty deep in the water.

Martin took the boat ten yards or so upstream and was back on the narrow ledge below my high bank with his gaff (one that would never break or twist). Two steady heaves with the rod brought the fish up on an even keel and Martin gaffed it amidships at the dorsal fin, saying it was the biggest fish he had ever gaffed. No ghastly terminal jagging.

We got it up on the top of the bank and banged it on the head as the cinema party came down to see how we had been getting on.

Fresh run "Spring" Cock Fish 59½lbs, 51½ inches long, girth 28½ inches, etc. Condition factor 43.6. No sea lice. Scales showed 4 years river life and 5 years sea life = 9 years old. Teeth fallen out or loose. Maiden fish. Some maiden! Playing time 9.40 p.m. to 10.20 p.m., 40 long, long minutes.

I was the guest of Mr and Mrs (later Dame Margery) A.B. Ashby and their son Dr Michael Ashby, my contemporary in the RAMC during the latter part of the Second World War. Mrs Corbett Ashby was the niece of Mr E.M. Corbett who had the Evanger fishing at that time and who invented Corbett's Condition Factor:

$$\frac{\text{Weight in lbs} \times 100{,}000}{\text{Length}^3 \text{ inches}}$$

should equal 40+ for a fish in top condition. Their kindness to an inexperienced but possibly slightly opinionated young man, was boundless.

Are there any lessons to be learnt from descriptions of battles against such big fish? The most obvious to me is that my big one and two of the three record fish caught by the ladies mentioned above were hooked after the sun (if any) had gone off the water, even Miss Davey's March fish. Dinner is the angler's enemy, high tea and late supper is the answer so far as fishing is concerned. Whether it is the answer as far as Life is concerned is another matter. If fishing is your life, even that is answered.

The best angler I ever met, L.R.N. (Lemon) Gray of the Torridge, told me this in the 1950s. Now in 1992 I know he was right.

So far as my own fish was concerned, it was never on less than 25 yards of line until it was well beaten and it was not gaffed until it was completely spent – both points due to the keeper's skill.

One of the signs of inexperience is a dreadful battle under the rod tip. Another is to fish the very best place half an hour too early.

J.R. Holden

THE BATTLE OF BOLSTADOYRI

A seasoned salmon-fisher, Terry Golding had several 20-pounders under his belt but still longed for something bigger. On the opening day of Norway's season his wish was certainly granted . . .

It was six years ago that I first started to hanker after one of those monster Norwegian salmon about which I'd heard so much. The vast majority of salmon fishermen consider themselves fortunate to encounter a 20lb fish. Those who have been lucky enough to connect with, and land, a 30lb salmon are a rare breed indeed. I have had several fish in the 20lb-plus class but my biggest, a 23-pounder on fly from Tweed, seemed a million miles from that coveted 30-pounder. So here I was again on June 1 and the start of a new salmon season on the Vosso.

Having arrived at the lodge I found to my dismay that I had drawn the short straw. I was to fish Oyne, which, by popular summary, was the beat you fished quickly before taking an early bath. This is a little unfair, since the records show that some very big fish have been taken from Oyne, but, like many myths in angling, if something is repeated often enough it becomes accepted. The beats rotate downstream each morning and evening and, as one young gillie pointed out, it would be a long time before I got to fish Rongon and Langhull, which were above where I was to start, and where I had calculated I would have the best chance of my 30-pounder.

By tradition most Norwegian rivers have rods out at one minute past midnight for half an hour or so and there is great rivalry to see which river will produce the first fish of the season. The Bolstad had already claimed that prize when, shortly after midnight and on his second cast, Minto Wilson landed a gleaming 30-pounder covered in sea-lice. This, then, was the first morning on the first day of the new season and with one fish already under our belts we all set off with great expectations.

Fishing began at 10 a.m. and after quickly fishing down the best bit of the right-hand bank my gillie, Brian Palmer, rowed us over to the far bank, where at the present water height the fish usually run up and rest. The current on the right bank was fierce, with foaming white water and rapids that I wanted nothing to do with.

When I first went to fish the Vosso I viewed with some trepidation a trip down the rapids that separate one pool from another. But after six years of watching friends careering down the rapids in hot pursuit of glass-case salmon I was now beginning to feel disappointed that I had not had a fish large enough to force me to do the same. Some anglers apparently insist on going down the rapids, regardless of the size of fish, just for the sheer thrill of the roller-coaster ride into the next pool. Taking one look at this particular splash-and-ride was enough to make me content to be fishing Oyne until the water dropped a little and I had a real chance of a fish on some of the other beats. Brian, on the other hand, had already announced that we were going to fish every inch of the far bank for every minute of the four-hour session and, if I didn't want to, then he would.

We started fishing about 10.25 a.m. The plan was to fish down the pool from the boat with a fly and then, if unsuccessful, try again with a spinning rod and spoon. I was using my Daiwa 16 ft Kevlar rod, Young's reel, and a Wet Cel II sinking line. The leader was somewhere in the high 20s breaking-strain and my fly was a two-inch black-and-yellow tube with a size 4 treble. Apart from the heavier leader, this is my standard autumn Tweed rig and the fishing method is exactly the same.

At 10.35 a.m. with the fly almost on the dangle, I had a solid pull and was into a fish. As salmon often do in the early stages of a fight, the fish came in towards the boat and seemed content merely to swim backwards and forwards while I heaved on the rod to tire it out as quickly as I could. Even at that stage it seemed like a good fish, and I did begin to wonder whether at last I was about to reach my "holy grail" of a 30lb salmon.

However, when he took off like a train in run after unstoppable run I began to think that all the techniques of "giving it some stick" and "being hard on it" could quickly be forgotten. Here was a fish that I was desperate not to lose, but the only possible response to the pulling I was experiencing was to hold on and pull back as hard as I could. Maybe this was my 30lb fish at last!

By a stroke of good luck Roger Hughes had been fishing the Bridge Pool below us with David Hodgkiss, one of the owners of the fishing. He had seen the rod bend almost at the minute the fish took, had hurried up to Oyne complete with camera, and was now reclining on a grassy bank smoking, taking pictures, and chatting to the gillie, who by now had worked the boat into a backwater where I thought I might be able to land the fish. I remember thinking they were being a bit casual about my fish and that someone ought to be making ready to receive my prize if I could just get him to come anywhere near the bank. The fish, however, had other ideas, and the sheer power of his runs was already making my arm ache. Roger and Brian had guessed that this was just the beginning of things and I could vaguely hear discussions about its being a big fish. Thinking that at last this must be my 30-pounder, I wondered why everyone appeared to be doing nothing but taking tea and eating my cake while I struggled with the fish – which surely by now, I thought, must be getting as tired as I was. I should have known that this was to be no ordinary battle when Brian, with classic understatement, said he did not think we were going to end the battle in Oyne. The fish must have overheard, because with one almighty run he was over to the far side of the river and into the fierce current. I was now being hurriedly pushed and rowed away from the bank and into that very same white water to follow the fish that by now was streaming the backing off my reel and heading for the Bridge Pool.

"We're going to have to go down," said Brian and I vaguely recall wondering how frightened I was going to be – but there was no time for this. Here was the fish of a lifetime running 50 yards away in an unstoppable rush and the only thing I could concentrate on was staying in touch with him. As we entered the rapids I tried to get as much line back on the reel as quickly as I could. I remember thinking there was no point worrying about the boat or where we were going with it. That was Brian's job, and I had no choice but to put my complete faith in his abilities. I must concentrate on the fish – but where was he, and why couldn't I reel in any faster? With the boat shooting down the white water I eventually managed to reel in all the loose line and found that the salmon was still on.

I was now playing the fish in the Bridge Pool and some 30 minutes after the battle had commenced, we had neither seen him nor had any sign that he was the least bit tired. David Hodgkiss had graciously retired from the pool but, along with his truly-meant "well done", could not resist the quip that after playing my fish for 15 minutes up and down his beat did I not think it was time I moved on down to interfere with someone else's fishing! Again I thought we might just be landing the fish in this pool – especially as the boat had been rowed close in to the bank – but now the fish was off again and we were into the rapids and following the fish under the famous Bolstadoyri Bridge.

Again the reel screamed and I was staring at yards of backing disappearing through the rod rings. And here was another problem; having again got on terms with him, the fish started to run back upstream on the right-hand bank. I was now playing the fish behind me and over Brian's shoulder! At least I could see that I still had my gillie with me after the last roller-coaster ride, but what on earth would we do if the fish decided to go back up? Even with an outboard motor we could not have followed. I honestly don't remember how we got out of that one and later I was staggered to learn that Brian had turned the boat through a full 360 degrees. As we turned, the fish must have come with us – an extraordinary feat of boatmanship and cool-headedness. What I do remember was having the boat pulled up the bank for the third time and thinking this really must be it – after 45 minutes this is where we are going to make our stand. But we still hadn't seen the fish and there was absolutely no sign that he was any less fresh than when I hooked him. To prove the point, the fish made a heart-stopping run right across the river.

Out again from the bank we were pushed, but the fish was now heading downstream and if he tried to go down into the fjord we would be in all sorts of trouble. The final set of rapids at this water height made the previous sets look like a mill-pond. There was only one possible way down and that was on the far side, where the current was not quite so fierce. In comparative terms this was still a joke as Roger's photographs subsequently were to show. However, this meant that we first had to get across the river at the very part where the stream starts to build up its greatest force and I was told later that to have achieved this in that current was a truly remarkable piece of strength and ghillying.

By the time we had bobbed around like a cork and followed the salmon down into the fjord I was again wondering where my fish was. When I finally got the line back on the reel the fish was not in the calm waters of the fjord but right in the middle of the most terrifying set of rapids and heading back up them! This was unbelievable! Where was all this nonsense about showing a salmon who's boss and giving it stick? For a few minutes I actually thought he was going back up to the lower Bridge Pool but then in another electrifying run he was back downstream and out into the fjord. Here was our chance. In the quieter water perhaps we could tow him around a bit or at least lead him into the bank. So here I was again, beached on a shingle bank, trying to keep the fish on a short line and vaguely aware that there were some 35 people behind me, watching and discussing the proceedings.

Brian was out of the boat and in the water with his gaff at the ready. This was it – and as I reeled in still further we saw our fish for the first time. Unfortunately, the fish saw us, too, took off again like a torpedo and forced us back into the boat to give chase in the fjord.

Apparently we became mere specks in the distance, and certainly, when the fish broke surface and stayed there with half its back out of the water, I began to wonder if this is what blue-water fishing must be like. Still I could not move him and rather than risk ripping the fly out of his mouth by forcing the fish along the surface I asked Brian to row towards him so that I could get some of the line back on my reel. The net result of this tactic was that the fish went down almost straight under the boat and was obviously trying to sound bottom.

This gave me another cause for concern. If the fish were exhausted, as I now began foolishly to hope, I would never be able to drag him up from the depths with the tackle I was using. I need have had no such fears, however, because the fish was soon off again and back up to the surface 30 yards away. "Try to stop him running like that by holding the rim of the reel," advised Brian. What he did not know, and could not see, was that I had actually been holding the reel handle and forcing the fish to take line against my reverse winding. This is a trick I often use, much to the alarm of various gillies I have fished with: but only when I believe a fish is tiring and always ready to let go of the handle if necessary. But this fish was so powerful that I could do nothing to stop him. My mouth was dry and Brian confirmed that he had the same trouble. The sheer tension and physical effort had affected us equally. A postcard from Bolstadoyri would have been out of the question as neither of us could have licked the stamp!

I was now absolutely exhausted. I was dropping the rod, and my reel-winding had seized up. "Couldn't you row nearer the fish," I remember asking Brian, "and perhaps gaff him into the boat?" This was desperation indeed, but a curt "No way," told me that I would have to keep going. As we had come down the final set of rapids I remember thinking that if this battle were to be truly memorable it should not be easy. I wanted it to be a hard fight; something to really remember. I was tired, then – but if I had known there was to be a further 30 minutes still to come I might have thought differently. I was now totally exhausted.

My arm had locked and I swear that it creaked every time I tried to raise or lower the rod. My left hand seemed detached from the rest of me and when I asked it to wind it seemed to respond only occasionally. I was done for.

When Brian eventually beached the boat we were on the far side of the fjord and as I started painfully to reel the fish in, he saw us again and would not come into the shallower water over a shingle bank. I heaved as hard as I could and tried to steer him to the gaff. Brian had gone in almost to his waist to assist, but when the first attempt failed and the fish took off again, I thought my strength would give out completely. I almost didn't care. Let him take line if he could. This was the king of fish in his own environment. If he broke free now, could I really complain after such a magnificent fight? I had had the ultimate fishing experience and the outcome now was almost an irrelevancy. Almost, but not quite. This was my fish and I wanted him!

The salmon was back on a short line and there was Brian with the fish expertly gaffed in the Norwegian way and bringing him ashore. Subsequent photos showed that I was still playing him on dry land before I dropped the rod, kissed the fish, and hugged the gillie in that order.

Back at the lodge I tried to clean my teeth to get the dryness from my mouth. I needed two hands to raise the toothbrush to my mouth. That evening I had to shave two-handed and I could not sleep on my right side for two nights. I had played the fish on a fly-rod through three beats, three sets of rapids and 1½ miles of river. The fish was shining silver, and covered with sea-lice. He was four feet long and had a 30-inch girth. The verified time of the encounter was 1 hour 15 minutes, and when put on the scales the fish weighed 49½lb. I and my fish were on the front page of the Norwegian national newspapers.

It is possibly the biggest fish ever landed from the Bolstad water on fly and certainly in recent years one of the biggest Atlantic salmon caught on a fly anywhere in the world. There have been bigger fish caught on different methods, and some even on fly, by the Dukes of Roxburghe and Westminster on the Alta; but I think it will do. At the time of writing my wife says I am a gibbering idiot. When I come out of shock perhaps I will be able to assess the whole thing better, but in the meantime I went trout fishing on the Pang on Sunday and lost three 1lb trout and was broken by a fourth. Those whom the Gods raise up . . .

Terry Golding in *Trout & Salmon*

An Early Start

No description of fishing on a Norwegian salmon river can rival this epic account by W. Bromley-Davenport of Fiva on the Rauma.

It is the unknown which constitutes the main charm and delight of every adult human creature's life from very childhood; which life from the beginning to the end is, I maintain, one continued gamble. Uncertainty is the salt of existence. I once emptied a large fish-pond, which, from my youth up, I had held in supreme veneration and angled in with awe, lest some of the monsters with which it was supposed to abound, especially one ferocious and gigantic pike which a six-foot gamekeeper gravely asserted to be as big as himself, and to have consumed endless broods of young ducks, should encounter me unawares, and the result was a great haul of small and medium-sized fish of all kinds, a few obese fat-headed carp, and the conspicuous absence of the monster pike.

I refilled the pond but never fished in it again; I knew what was in it, and also what was *not* in it. Its mystery, and with it its glory, had departed. So it is with shooting – I hate to know how many pheasants there are in a wood, how many coveys in a partridge beat, how many birds in a covey. So it is, of course, with everything else in life. Whatever is reduced to a certainty ceases to charm, and, but for the element of risk or chance –

uncertainty in short – not only every sport or amusement, but even every operation and transaction of this world, would be tame and irksome. If we foreknew the result we would seldom do anything, and would eventually be reduced to the condition of the bald, toothless, toeless, timid, sedentary, and incombative "man of the future" foreshadowed recently by a very advanced writer. How few would ever marry a wife if the recesses of her mind were previously laid as bare as my fish-pond! And how few women would accept a husband under similar circumstances! So that the elimination of the element of uncertainty would perhaps lead to universal celibacy. Still possessing it however, and far from any approximation to this latter result, let me sing the praises of that sport which ranks next to fox-hunting in its utter absence of certainty – the prince and king of all the angling domain – salmon-fishing. Delightful in itself, this regal sport conducts its worshippers into the grandest and wildest scenes of nature, to one of which I will at once ask my reader to accompany me.

We will imagine that it is the middle of June, and that London has begun to be as intolerable as it usually becomes at that season, and that he is willing to fly with me across the sea and to settle down for a space in a Norwegian valley, and, surrounded by scenery unsurpassed in its abrupt wildness by anything to be seen even in that wildest of wild countries, survey salmon-fishing from an Anglo-Norwegian sportsman's point of view. Having with more or less discomfort safely run the gauntlet of that most uncertain and restless of oceans, the North Sea, we land at the head of the Romsdal Fjord, and after about an hour's carriole drive are deposited, stunned and bewildered by the eccentricities which stupendous and impossible Nature has erected all around us, at the door of a clean, pine-built, white-painted house, in the midst of what looks like the happy valley of Rasselas; surrounded by bright green meadows, walled in by frowning impracticable precipices 2,000 feet high at their lowest elevation, and over 4,000 at their highest, at the top of which, opposite the windows to the south-west, even as exclusive mortals garnish their walls with broken bottles, so Nature appears to have wished to throw difficulties in the way of some gigantic trespasser by placing a fearful chevaux-de-frise of strange, sharp, jagged, uncouth and fantastic peaks, which baffle all description in their dreamy grotesqueness. These are called by the natives "Troll tinderne," i.e. "witch peaks," or "sorcerers' seats." A stone dropped from the top would touch nothing for 1,500 feet, and thence to the bottom would lose but little velocity, so near the perpendicular is the rest of the descent. Below the steepest portion is a long stony slope having the appearance of a landslip, formed by some of the broken and pulverised *debris* of many a colossal crag, whose granite foundations Time having besieged ever since the Flood, has at length succeeded in undermining, and which has then toppled over with a report like a salvo of 10,000 80-pounders, filling the valley – here two miles wide – with a cloud of fine dust resembling thick smoke, and yet, after scattering huge splinters far and wide, has still retained sufficient of its original and gigantic self to roll quietly through the dwarf birch and sycamore wood at the bottom, crushing flat and obliterating trees thick as a man's body in girth, and leaving a gravel walk behind it broad as a turnpike road, till it subsides into some sequestered hollow, where, surrounded by trees no taller than itself, it will reclothe itself with moss and grow grey again for another 4,000 years or so. The prevailing opinion among the peasants is that this wall being very narrow, and its other side equally precipitous, some day or other the whole precipice will fall bodily into the valley; and in this theory they are strengthened by the fact, or tradition, that at a certain time during the winter the moon can be seen to shine through an orifice situated half-way up its face, undiscernible save when lighted up in this manner. This is a pretty belief, and I am sorry that my telescope, with which I have narrowly scanned every cranny, does not confirm it. The fact is possible all the same; but the convulsion of nature which they anticipate does not follow as a matter of course, and in my opinion the "trolls" will sit undisturbed on their uncomfortable seats till some general crash occurs, which will convolve other valleys than this, and higher peaks than theirs. However:

> Mountains have fallen,
> Leaving a gap in the clouds,

and it is possible that this accident may occur. I only hope that I may be non-resident at my Norway home when it does. Here and there in nooks and crannies rest large patches of drift-snow which, when loosened and released by the summer heat, fall down the sides in grand thunderous cascades, bringing with them rocks and stones, with occasional fatal results to the cattle and sheep feeding in apparent security in the woods below. Opposite the Troll tinderne on the north-eastern side of the valley the Romsdal Horn rears its untrodden head. It falls so sheer and smooth towards the river that it affords no resting-place for the snow, consequently no avalanches fall on this side; but occasionally, as from the Troll tinderne, a huge rock is dislodged by time and weather; and sometimes I have seen one of these come down from the very top, and marked its progress by the slight puffs of smoke which long before the report reaches the ear are plainly to be seen, as in its successive leaps it comes in contact with the mountain side; and the length of time which elapses between the first reverberation that makes one look up when the solid mass takes its first spring from the summit, and the last grape-shot clatter of its fragments at the foot of the Horn, gives me some idea of the terrific proportions of this wonderful rock. Sometimes I can hardly help, as I look up at its awful sides, giving it personal identity and the attributes of life – regarding it with a sort of terror, and with a humble desire somehow to *propitiate* it, as a merciful giant who respects and pities my minute life, and disdains to put his foot upon me or crush me with one of his granite thunderbolts.

In my youth I tried to gain its summit, where tradition says there is a lake on which floats a golden bowl. I failed miserably; but have no doubt that with proper appliances, which I had not, some skilled Alpine climber would succeed. One such, alas! came out some two years ago with such appliances, and the strong resolve of youth and abounding strength, steadfastly purposed to solve the mystery. He only attained the deeper mystery of death; not in the attempt, but drowned deplorably by the upsetting of a boat which he had engaged to cross the Fjord (being unwilling, in his eager haste to reach the scene of his proposed adventure, to wait even a day for the regular steamer which would have conveyed him safely) close to the shore at the very mouth of the Rauma river. It is this river Rauma out of which I want my reader to catch a salmon, or see me catch one. It flows down the middle of the valley, not as Scotch rivers, London or Dublin porter-hued, but clear, bright, and translucent as crystal.

Here, amid such scenes, with this glorious stream rushing tumultuously in a sort of semicircle round me, thus giving me some half-a-dozen salmon pools, each within about 200 yards from the house, have I provided myself with a dwelling and an estate – partly for sake of the sport, and partly to have another string to my bow – some refuge even in republican Norway from the possible legislation of constitutional England, where inability to pay the heavy bill for "unearned increment," which has in my case been running for some 900 years, may cause my family estates to be handed over to somebody else. It is too late tonight – we will fish tomorrow – we are tired. The wooden walls and floors of the house still heave and sway with recollections of the German Ocean. We will sleep the sleep of Tories and the just.

"Klokken Fem i Morgen, Ole!" "Five o'clock tomorrow morning, Ole!" was my last instruction to my faithful boatman and gaffer yesterday evening, and, sure enough, as I jump up instinctively a quarter of an hour before the appointed time, I see him outside my window busying himself with my rod, while my reel gives out short periodical sounds, like the call of a corn-crake, as he passes the line through each successive ring. One glance at the sky is enough – clear blue and cloudless, fresh and cool, but no wind – a slight mist hangs half-way up the Troll tinderne; below it all is clear, though heavily laden with moisture, and in dark contrast with the bright sun above, which is already, and has been for some hours, playing among the topmost peaks, and gladdening the stony-hearted rocks themselves.

Brief – oh, brief is the process of adornment and ablution in the india-rubber bath, for my soul is very eager for the fray; and the day will evidently be a hot one, rendering it impossible to fish after nine o'clock, when the sun will be on the river. A hot cup of coffee – made as Norwegians can make it and we can't – and a scrap of biscuit occupies about one minute of time in consumption, and the next I am striding away towards "Aarnehoe," my upper and best pool, brushing away the heavy dew from the grass and dwarf juniper bushes, and drinking in life and health from every inspiration of the fresh morning air. My little boat tosses like a nutshell among the high waves of the turbulent stream as it is swept across to the other side of the river, where a romantic glade conducts me to the wooden bridge, two planks wide, which crosses a divergent stream and leads me to the now almost dreaded pool. A keen salmon-fisher will understand me and forgive me if I fail to do justice to the impressions, the hopes, and the fears of the hour. The field of battle is before me, white and tumultuous at the head, smooth and black in the middle, full of surging bubbles, like the ebullitions of millions of soda-water bottles from the bottom, clear, swift, and transparent at the tail.

In spite of the roar of the foss in my ears, I am under the impression of perfect stillness and *silence* in the objects round me, so wild, solitary, and secluded is the spot; no habitation or trace of man, save my boatman's presence, desecrates the scene. My eyes are fixed with a sort of fascination on the water, whose swift but calmly flowing surface remains unruffled, unbroken as yet by the dorsal fin of any scaly giant, and gives no evidence of the life it contains. It is the Unknown! and as Ole unmoors the boat I confess that a feeling of trepidation seizes me – a feeling difficult to define – of anticipated pleasure mingled with respect for the power and strength of the unseen and unknown antagonist with whom I am about to grapple, and making me entertain no boastful confidence in the result of the struggle which will forthwith commence between us. But all is prepared. Ole, smiling and expectant, holds the boat, which dances a little in the swell, steady for me to enter; and, with his cheerful but invariable platitude: "Nu skal ve har store fisken" ("Now we will have a big fish"), takes his place and rows me up under the very breakers of the foss. A few short preliminary throws give me the requisite length of line to reach the smooth black water, full of submerged eddies, beyond the influence of the force of the torrent, and I begin; once – twice – thrice does the fly perform its allotted circuit and return to me unmolested; but the fourth time, just as I am in the act of withdrawing it from the water for another cast, the bowels of the deep are agitated, and, preceded by a wave impelled and displaced by his own bulk, flounders heavily and half out of the water a mighty salmon. Broad was he, and long to boot, if I may trust an eye not unaccustomed to such apparitions; his white and silvery side betokening his recent arrival from the German Ocean, the slightly roseate hues of his back and shoulders giving unfailing evidence, if corroborative evidence were wanting, after one glimpse of that spade-like tail, of a "salmo salar" of no common weight and dimensions. My heart – I confess it leaped up to my very mouth – but he has missed the fly, and an anxious palpitating five minutes which I always reluctantly allow must elapse before I try him again. They are gone, and in trembling hope – with exactly the same length of line, and the boat exactly in the same place, Ole having fixed the spot to an inch by some mysterious landmarks on the shore – I commence my second trial. Flounce! There he is! not so demonstrative this time – a boil in the water and a slight plash, as the back fin cuts the surface, that's all; but something tells me this is the true attack. A slight, but sharp turn of the wrist certifies the fact, and brings – oh, moment of delight! my line taut and my rod bent to a delicious curve.

Habet! he has it! Now, Ole! steadily and slowly to the shore! He is quite quiet as yet, and has scarcely discovered the singular nature and properties of the insect he has appropriated, but swims quietly round and round in short circles, wondering no doubt, but so far unalarmed. I am only too thankful for the momentary respite, and treat him with the most respectful gentleness, but a growing though scarcely perceptible increase of the strain on my rod bends it gradually lower and lower until the reel begins to give out its first slow music. My fingers are on the line to give it the slight resistance of friction, but the speed increases too rapidly for me to bear them there long, and I withdraw them just in time to save their being cut to the bone in the tremendous rush which follows. Whizz–z–z! up the pool he goes! the line scattering the spray from the surface in a small fountain, like the cut-water of a Thames steamer. And now a thousand fears assail me – should there be one defective strand in my casting-line, one doubtful or rotten portion of my head-line, should anything *kink* or foul, should the hook itself (as sometimes happens) be a bad one – farewell, oh giant of the deep, for ever! *Absit omen*! all is well as yet, that rush is over. He has a terrible length of my line out, but he is in a safe part of the pool and rather disposed to come back to me, which gives me the opportunity, which I seize eagerly, of reeling up my line. The good-tempered, reasonable monster! But steady! there is a limit to his concessions. No further will he obey the rod's gentle dictation.

Two rebellious opiniative kicks nearly jerk my arms out of

the shoulder joints, and then down he goes to the bottom. Deep in the middle of the pool he lies, obdurate, immovable as a stone. There must he not remain! That savage strength must not be husbanded. I re-enter the boat, and am gently rowed towards him, reeling up as I advance. He approves not this, as I expected. He is away again into the very midst of the white water, till I think he means to ascend the foss itself – hesitates irresolute there a moment, then back again down the middle of the stream like a telegraphic message. "Row ashore, Ole! Row for life! for now he means mischief!" Once in the swift water at the tail of the pool he will try not only my reel, but my own wind and condition to boot; for down he *must* go now, weighed he but a poor five pounds; once out of this pool and there is nothing to stop him for 300 yards. We near the shore, and I spring into the shallow water and prance and bound after him with extravagant action, blinding myself with the spray which I dash around me. Ah! well I know and much I fear this rapid! The deep water being on the other side of the river, the fish invariably descend there, and from the wide space intervening, too deep for man to wade in, too shallow for fish to swim in, and too rough for boat to live in, the perturbed fisherman must always find an awful length of line between him and his fish, which, however, he can in no way diminish till he arrives considerably lower down, where the river is narrower. Many a gallant fish has by combination of strength and wile escaped me here. Many a time has my heart stood still to find that my line and reel have suddenly done the same – what means it? In the strength of that mighty torrent can mortal fish rest? Surely, but he must have found a shelter somewhere? Some rock behind which to lie protected from the current! I must try and move him! Try and move the world! A rock is indeed there and the line is round it, glued to it immovably by weight of water. It is *drowned*. But he, the fish! seaward may he now swim half a league away, or at the bottom of the next pool may be rubbing some favourite fly against the stones. Nay – but see! the line runs out still, with jerks and lifelike signs. Hurrah! we have not lost him yet. Oh, dreamer, ever hoping to the last, no more life there than in a galvanised corpse, whose spasmodic actions the line is imitating! It is bellying deep in the stream, quivering and jerking, slacking and pulling as the current dictates, creating movements which, through the glamour of a heated imagination, seem as the struggles of a mighty fish.

That fish, that fly, and perhaps that casting-line shall that fisherman never see again? Such doom and such a result may the gods now avert! My plungings and prancings have brought me to the foot of my wooden bridge – made very high on purpose to avoid the period above described (and for the same purpose I keep well behind or upstream of my fish) – which I hurry over with long strides, and many an anxious glance at my ninety or hundred yards of line waving and tossing through the angry breakers encompassed by a hundred dangers. With rod high held and panting lungs I spring from the bridge, and blunder as I best may along the stony and uneven bank for another hundred yards with unabated speed. I am saved! Safe floats the line in the deep but still rapid and stormy water beyond the extremest breaker, and here, fortunately for me, my antagonist slackens his speed, having felt the influence of a back-water which guides him rather back to me, and I advance in a more rational manner, and in short sobs regain the breath of life; but one aching arm must still sustain the rod on high while the other reels up as for very existence. Forward, brave Ole! and have the next boat ready in case the self-willed monster continues his reckless course, which he most surely will; for, lo! in one fiery whizz out goes all the line which that tired right hand had so laboriously reclaimed from the deep, and down, proudly sailing mid-stream, my temporary tyrant recommences his hitherto all-triumphant progress. I follow as I best may, but now, having gained the refuge of the boat, a few strokes of Ole's vigorous boat-compelling oars recover me the line I had lost, and land me on the opposite bank, where, with open water before me for some distance, I begin for the first time to realise the possibility of victory. However:

Much hath been done, but more remains to do,

but of a less active, more ponderous, painstaking patience-trying description. The long deep stream of Langhole is before me in which he will hang – does hang, will sulk – does sulk, and has to be roused by stones cast in above, below, and around him. As yet, I have never seen him since his first rise, but Ole, who has climbed the bank above me, and from thence can see

27

far into the clear bright water, informs me that he gets an occasional glimpse of him, and that he is "meget meget store," or very, very big. My heart – worn and weary as it is with the alternations of hope and fear – re-flutters, at this intelligence, for I know that Ole is usually a fish-decrier or weight-diminisher. All down the length of Langhole, 250 yards by the tale, does he sullenly bore, now and then taking alarming excursions far away to the opposite shore, oftener burying himself deep in the deepest water close at my feet; but at length he resolves on more active operations, and, stimulated by the rapid stream at the tail of Langhole, takes advantage thereof and goes down bodily to the next pool, Tofte. I have no objection to this, even if I had a voice in the matter; I have a flat smooth meadow to race over, the stream has no hidden rocky dangers, so, like swift Camilla, I scour the plain till the deeper and quieter recesses of Tofte afford an asylum for the fish and breathing time to myself. Here, I hope, but hope in vain, to decide the combat; occasionally I contrive to gain the advantage of a short line, but the instant he perceives the water shoaling away he bores indignant, and spurns the shallow. The engagement has now lasted more than an hour, and my shoulders are beginning to ache, and yet no symptoms of submission on the part of my adversary; on the contrary, he suddenly reassumes the offensive, and with a rush which imparts such rotatory motion to my reel as to render the handle not only intangible but actually invisible, he forsakes the delights of Tofte, and continues his course down the river. I must take to the boat again (I have one on every pool) and follow, like a harpooner towed by a whale. The river widens below Tofte, and a short swift shallow leads to the next pool, Langholmen, or Long Island. I have a momentary doubt whether to land on the island or on the opposite side where there is a deeper but swifter pool, towards which the fish is evidently making. I decide at once, but decide wrong – which is better, however, than not deciding at all – and I land on Langholmen, into whose calm flowing water I had fondly hoped that incipient fatigue would have enticed my fish, and find him far over in the opposite pool with an irreconcilable length of line doubtfully connecting us. It is an awful moment! It he goes up stream now, I am lost – that is to say, my fish is – which in my present frame of mind is the same thing; no line or hook would ever stand the strain of that weight of water. But, no, mighty as he is, he is mortal, and but a fish after all, and even his giant strength is failing him, and inch by inch and foot by foot he drops down the stream, and as he does so the reel gradually gains on him, till at the tail of Langholmen I have the delight of getting, for the first time since he rose, a fair sight of his broad and shining bulk, as he lies drifting sulkily and indolently down the clear shallows. I exult with the savage joy which the gladiator may have felt when he perceived for the first time the growing weakness of his antagonist, and I set no bounds to my estimate of his size. Fifty pounds at least! I proclaim loudly to Ole, is the very minimum of the weight I give him. Ole smiles and shakes his head detractingly. The phlegmatic, unsympathetic, realistic wretch! On I go, however, wading knee-deep over the glancing shingle. The lowest pool, and my last hope before impassable rapids, Laerneset, is before me, and after wading waist-deep across the confluent stream at the end of the island, I gain the commanding bank and compel my now amenable monster into the deep, still water, out of the influence of the current. And now, feebler and feebler grow his rushes, shorter and shorter grows the line, till mysterious whirlpools agitate the calm surface, and at last, with a heavy, weary plunge, upheaves the spent giant, and passive, helpless, huge, "lies floating many a rood."

Still even now his *vis inertiae* is formidable, and much caution and skill have to be exercised in towing that vanquished hull into port, lest with one awkward heavy roll, or one feeble flop of that broad, spreading tail, he may tear away hook or hold, and so rob me at last of my hardly-earned victory. No such heartbreaking disaster awaits me. Ole, creeping and crouching like a deer-stalker, extends the fatal gaff, buries it deep in the broad side, and drags him, for he is, in very sooth, too heavy to lift, unwilling and gasping to the shore, where, crushing flat the long grass, he flops and flounders till a merciful thwack on the head from the miniature policeman's staff, which I always carry for this purpose, renders him alike oblivious and insensible to past suffering or present indignity. And now I may calmly survey his vast proportions and speculate on the possibility of his proving too much for my weighing machine, which only gives information up to fifty pounds. To a reasonable-sized fish I can always assign an approximate weight, but this one takes me out of the bounds of my calculation, and being as sanguine as

Ole is the reverse, I anxiously watch the deflection of the index as Ole, by exercising his utmost strength, raises him by a hook through his under jaw from the sound, with a wild sort of hope still possessing me (foolish though I inwardly feel it to be) that the machine won't weigh him.

Forty-five anyhow he *must* be! Yes, he is! no, he ain't! Alas! after a few oscillations it settles finally at forty-three pounds, with which decision I must rest content, and I *am* content. I give way to senseless manifestations of extravagant joy, and even Ole relaxes. Early as it is, it is not too early for a Norwegian to drink spirits, and I serve him out a stiff dram of whisky on the spot, which he tosses down raw without winking, while I dilute mine from the river, for this ceremony, on such occasions, must never be neglected. "Now, Ole, shoulder the prey as you best can, and home to breakfast;" for now, behold, from behind the giant shoulder of the Horn bursts forth the mighty sun himself! illuminating the very depths of the river, sucking up the moisture from the glittering grass, and drying the tears of the blue bells and the dog violets, and calling into life the myriads whose threescore years and ten are to be compressed into the next twelve hours. Yet how they rejoice! Their songs of praise and enjoyment positively din in my ears as I walk home, rejoicing, too, after my Anglo–Saxon manner, at having killed something, fighting the battle over again in extravagantly bad Norse to Ole, who patiently toils on under the double burden of the big fish and my illiterate garrulity. In short I am thoroughly happy – self-satisfied and at peace with all mankind. I have succeeded, and success usually brings happiness; everything looks bright around me, and I thankfully compare my lot with that of certain pallid, flaccid beings, whom my mind's eye presents to me stewing in London, and gasping in midsummer torment in the House of Commons. A breakfast of Homeric proportions (my friend and I once ate a seven-pound grilse and left nothing even for a dog) follows this morning performance. Will my reader be content to rest after it, smoke a pipe, bask in the sun (he won't stand that long, for the Norway sun is like the kitchen fire of the gods), and possibly, after Norwegian custom, take a mid–day nap?

from *Sport* 1885

A FIFTY-POUNDER-PLUS

I shall never know the true weight of the biggest salmon I have ever caught. That it weighed more than 50 pounds is definitely sure. For the only scales in the lodge weighed no more than this and the fish certainly did – by several pounds. According to the Sturdy scale a fish of 52 inches should weigh about 60 pounds!

The fish took a 9/0 single hook Thunder and Lightning. This was attached to the line by a cast of the heaviest gut which it was possible to buy. Tested by attaching the hook to the rail of the verandah and pulling, it only passed as fit if neither the cast nor the line could be broken nor the iron of the fly be straightened.

I went by myself to fish a pool known as "Solsken" (which means Sunshine) off one of the platforms which are built right across this un-wadeable, un-boatable river Aaro. I had hardly got my line out when the fish took and very quickly came almost to the surface as he tried to turn away with the fly.

If one of these big fish is ever allowed to turn side-on in these powerful streams of the Aaro a breakage is certain. The only way in which they can be killed is by the angler getting directly straight above them and pulling them so hard that they cannot turn side-on.

This I proceeded to do. I quickly ran along the platform until I was directly above the fish and then, with a 16ft greenheart bent nearly double, began to pull as hard as possible. For about forty minutes the salmon struggled to get turned sideways but I

31

had sufficent strength to keep him directly below me as I edged along the platform towards the shore. Happily the river here lapped onto a shingle beach and with very little difficulty I got the fish to swim up almost on to it. He was far too big to catch by the tail so I slid my fingers into his gills and pulled him up the beach and killed him with a big stone.

Very big fish suffer from being too big. Their gills are comparatively too small for their body size and weight. Unable to acquire sufficient oxygen in their bloodstream they cannot utilise the latent energy stored in their tissues and it is this, not tiredness, which causes them to give up the struggle.

It always sounds very grand to say, "I caught a fish of over 50 pounds on a fly and landed it alone without a gaff." In truth, when once you understand the technique of playing big fish in heavy water it is really quite simple.

Richard Waddington

SCOTLAND

LANDING THE RECORD TAY SALMON
(64LB)

On the evening of 7 October, 1922, after a rather strenuous day's fishing, which resulted in the capture of three fine salmon, we determined to finish the day on the river. It was the last evening before the hour changed, therefore we were anxious to make the most of our time.

We amounted to Father and myself, he rowing, as Melvin, the boatman, had knocked off at 5 pm. After towing up the boat we started harling, using two rods, the fly "Wilkinson" on the right, and the dace, which I was plying on the left. The bait was exceptionally well put on with an attractive curl on its tail and spinning along briskly as only Malloch's minnows can spin.

A few turns at the top of "Boat Pool" as the sun dipped down behind the hill brought no result. Immediately above the "Bargie" stone Father remarked that we should "see him here": scarcely were the words spoken when a sudden "rug" and "screech" of the reel brought my rod in an upright position. He was hooked! The bait he seized with no unusual violence at 6.15 pm and thinking him an ordinary-sized fish, we tried to encourage him to play into the back water behind "Bargie", a large boulder. Our hopes, however, upon this point were soon "barkin' and fleein'". Realizing evidently that something was amiss, he made a headlong dash for freedom and flew (I can apply no other term to his sudden flight.) Down the river he went in mid-stream, taking a run of about 500 yards before stopping, at the same time carrying with him about 150 yards of line. Quick as lightning the boat was turned, heading down-stream, and soon we overtook and got him under hand and within reasonable distance.

Heading for the north bank, we were in the act of landing about 200 yards above the Bridge when he came practically to the end of the boat[1]. Scenting danger ahead, he again ran out of reach. Leaving the boat, we followed him down, and as chance would have it he passed between the north pier and the bank when going under the Bridge[2], otherwise we would have been in a dreadful hole.

Not once did he show himself, so we were mercifully kept in blissful ignorance of the monster we were fated to fight to the death.

About 200 yards below the Bridge Father thought it advisable to fetch the boat, as the fish obstinately kept out in the current. Evidently our progress downstream was farther than Father had anticipated, as I immediately got into hot water; "dinna lat the beast flee doon the watter like that, 'ummin".

With few remarks and much hand-spitting[3] we again boarded the boat, this time keeping in mid-stream for fully half an hour. As time went on the strain of this was getting beyond us; the fish remained stationary and sulked. Then we endeavoured to humour and encourage him to the Murthly bank, but he absolutely refused to move.

Again gradually crossing the river we tried to bring him into the backwater at the junction half-way down to Sparrowmuir, where a small breakwater juts out. Again no luck attended our movements in this direction, though we worked with him for a considerable time. Eventually we re-crossed over close to the island. By this time darkness had come down, and we could see the trees on the island silhouetted against the sky.

We had hoped by the light of the moon to find a suitable landing-place, but unfortunately a dark cloud obscured her. The fish kept running out a few paces, then returning, but long intervals were spent without even a movement. He inclined always downstream, until the middle of the island was reached, and the light in the cottage window at Sparrowmuir blinked

[1]Had a third party been at hand he might have been gaffed within ten minutes.
[2]Bridge has two piers, three divisions.
[3]An unconscious habit of Father's when excited.

cheerily across the river.

By this time my left arm ached so much with the weight of the rod that it felt paralysed, but I was determined that whatever happened nothing would induce me to give in. "Man if only the Laird or the Major had ta'en him I wouldna' ha' been sae ill aboot it." Encouraging remarks such as those I swallowed silently. Once I struck the nail on the head by remarking that if I successfully grassed this fish he must give me a new frock. "Get ye the fish landed first and syne we'll see aboot the frock," was the reply. (Nevertheless I have kept him to his word and the frock has been ordered.) By this time we were prepared to spend the night on the Island.

Tighter, and tighter still, the order came, until the tension was so great that no ordinary line could have stood the test for any length of time. It says much for both line and tackle in playing such an important part. Nearer and nearer he came until I was ordered to change my seat to the bow of the boat, and by keeping the rod upright Father was thus enabled to feel with the gaff the knot at the junction of line and cast. Having gauged the distance, the remainder was easy. I wound the reel steadily out until only the cast (length of cast, three and three-quarter yards) was left. One awful moment of suspense followed – then the gaff went in successfully, which brought him to the side of the boat. A second lift (no small weight, over half a hundredweight) brought him over the end into the floor of the boat, Father, out of puff, half sitting on top of him.

Reaching for Mr Moir's "Nabbie", I made a somewhat feeble attempt to put him out of pain, and was afterwards accused of "knockin' oot ane o' the puir beast's een!" It is unnecessary to describe the homeward journey; I was ordered to remain in the boat while Father towed it up. We were met at the Bridge by the old lady, my mother, who was considerably relieved to see us back; her greeting showed how perturbed and anxious she had been during our absence: "Guid sakes I thocht ye were baith i' the watter!"

No time was lost in administering a stiff dose of "toddy" which I considered a necessary and well-earned "nightcap". Thus ended a "red-letter" day in the annals of the famous Glendelvine beat of the River Tay.

Georgina Ballantine in *The Fishing Gazette*.

CASSLEY: JUNE, 1957

I was working at my desk one afternoon, just after lunch, when my keeper Willie MacKay called in to say that the river was in perfect order and suggested that it would be well worth while trying a cast. I agreed to meet him at 4 pm at the Old Post Office, Rosehall, on the right bank of the river just across the bridge, because I knew the home bank was being fished by friends of my father's.

It was a fine summer afternoon, cloudy but dry with a light westerly wind. I, therefore, just put on a pair of wellingtons, grabbed my hat and shoved a fly box in my pocket, then drove over to the Post Office, where Willie was waiting with the rods. We decided to walk up to the Round Pool, about half a mile upstream, and then fish our way back down to the car.

The rod Willie had taken for me was a light, 14-foot spliced greenheart, with a greased line, a rod I used in low water and when fishing in the evening often fished on for sea trout with it at night. When I was halfway up to the Round Pool, I suddenly remembered that I only had a very light cast on. I turned to Willie and said, "I hope you have some casts with you," and explained why. After rummaging around in his pockets he gave a guilty look and said, "I am afraid I haven't." At that stage there was no point in turning back; I would just have to make the best of it as it was entirely my fault for not taking a spool with me.

On arrival at the pool, I sat down to study my dilemma and think out a plan how to overcome it. It transpired that I had a pretty worn 8 lb breaking strain cast with a dropper. I decided I would cut off the dropper and put on a no.9 Blue Charm dressed on a Wilson low water hook on the tail, and suggested that Willie should fish down behind me with a larger fly, as the river was fairly high.

When I was about halfway down the pool I got a firm pull and having struck, knew I was into a good fish. After about 15 minutes a beautiful sea-liced 16 lb salmon was lying on the bank. As time was wearing on I told Willie to fish out the rest of the pool and then fish the Run, whilst I went down to the Upper Platform Pool round the corner some 200 yards away.

When I got to the pool, I fished it down very quietly and opposite the platform on the left bank saw a large quiet boil behind my fly, but no contact. I moved upstream some five yards and came down over the spot again and immediately felt a slight pull, as the fish took. On striking, I saw an enormous swirl and knew I was in contact with a really big fish. Just my luck, I thought, to hook a monster when I had a tattered cast on, but there was nothing I could do but hope and pray that the fish behaved itself.

Once again my luck was out as the fish did anything but behave. It tore down to the tail of the pool with my reel screaming, turned quickly and roared back upstream, jumping three times successively high in the air as it passed me, and moved right up into the fast water at the neck of the pool. I retrieved my line with trepidation, but luckily the fish was still on and it began to settle and sulk.

Willie by this time, having caught an 11 lb fish in the Round, had been fishing the Tail of the Run when he saw the commotion and came running to help. He arrived huffing and puffing under the weight of 27 lbs of fish, rod, net, etc., and being a heavy man was completely out of breath. He was just about to ask me what size fish I had on, when my fish jumped once again high in the air, right in front of him. To say the least he was speechless, because a 15 to 18 lb is a good fish for the Cassley, a 20 lb-plus fairly rare, and a 30 lb unheard of. At that precise moment there is no doubt that we both knew that the fish on the end of my line would be the record fish for this river, a glance between us said it all. Whether we would ever land it was another matter.

After this jump, the fish moved out into the centre of the

pool and the line jerk–jerked as it continually shook its head, then it came to the surface and wallowed as it tried to slap the line with its spade–like tail. Still the hook hold held and the cast unbelievably stayed intact. Then slowly but surely the fish moved into the deepest part of the pool under a protruding rock ledge, close to the bank we were standing on at the tail of the pool, and I knew that if my taut cast came in contact with the sharp jagged rock edge, it would be curtains. To make things even worse, there was a film of foam in the backwater close to the ledge, and under that the fish was determined to stay.

At long last Willie broke the silence and said, "I have a gaff in my game bag. If you can raise the fish to the surface I might have a chance to get it, but if I try to net the fish I will never be able to see it under the scum." Reluctantly I agreed, and Willie positioned himself as close to the edge of the ledge as he could. Obviously, the amount of pressure I could exert with my tattered cast and the fear of rubbing the cast on the ledge, was extremely limited. I was even frightened to cough, let alone exert force and by now there was an audience on the other bank, which made one's nerves even more frayed. Luckily, however, we both kept cool, not a word passing between us, each relying on the other.

At long last the tell–tale swirls on the surface indicated that the fish was tiring and shortly afterwards I managed to ease its head close to the surface and swing it towards Willie, who made no mistake.

After 25 minutes' hard battle and many a missed heartbeat, a fine 31½ lb cock fish lay shining on the bank. It was a record for the Cassley and that record still stands today.

I can assure you that whenever I go fishing now I always make sure I have a spool of nylon in my pocket, and to make doubly sure leave three spools of differing strengths in the pocket of my car at the very start of the fishing season. Once bitten, twice shy!!

Neil Graesser

July 1936

I was fishing Beat 3 (upper river) on the Helmsdale accompanied by my cousin Nigel Turner and ghillie Donald Munro, a man of strange and unpredictable habits. I was fishing a pool called Dalbuie. The river was at normal summer level and I was armed with a 14-foot Hardy split cane rod, 1 × gut cast and a size 6 or 8 Thunder and Lightning double-knotted fly.

At the best taking spot, where the water ran fairly swiftly over a deeper lie I hooked a fish that felt fairly heavy. Nothing much happened for quite a time. He merely cruised around in the area of the lie. I exerted as much pressure as I dared from below him and eventually he sailed upstream through fast shallow water making one or two powerful surges. Then he returned to the lie and after a bit more sulking he repeated this with me pulling against him from just downstream.

After some time he came up to just below the surface and lay almost stationary, and this is when the drama began. I was standing in about a foot of water on a smooth peat shelf and within reach with the gaff of the still motionless fish. I called to Donald for the gaff. "Wait till I put off ma boots" was the exasperating reply and he sat down and removed his large hobnailed boots. Eventually he waddled out to me but just as he reached me he put his wobbly foot into a deep hole in the peat and staggered. I grabbed him by the scruff of the neck and held on but the jerk caused the fish to shoot off down to the deep lie. We struggled out and I got down level with the fish.

I was now on level grass with about three foot sheer drop to the water. When I tried to lift the fish to the surface he came up but being completely "done" he started to roll downstream in the fast running glide to the tail of the pool. I told Donald to get down to the shallows leading to the pool below and I would try to steer the fish to him. Just as Donald reached the middle of the shallows he put one of his corns, about which he often moaned, on a sharp stone and subsided onto his knees giving an agonised yell. The fish was smack on target and went through his legs. I flung the rod on the shingle and ran. The long wooden-handled gaff was tumbling down the shallows just behind the fish. I grabbed it and made a desperate swipe at the fish just as it reached the deep water of the "Duchess" pool. Fortunately I connected and dragged it out.

The contest had lasted over three-quarters of an hour and the fish weighed 22½ lb, reasonably fresh but not bad at all. We had a large slug of whisky and I gave Donald one to help his corns. Looking back on it, it was hilarious – in fact Nigel, always a giggler, went on laughing for the rest of the day.

Douglas Pilkington

A Foul-Hooked "Almost"
40-Pounder

To my eternal regret I have never caught a 40 lb fish in Britain. The nearest I have come to this is a fish taken on a No .6 Garry Dog in, appropriately enough, the Dog Pool on the Inverness-shire Garry. This lovely fish was hooked when the river was running somewhat above summer level at the end of May. It made a beautiful rise and immediately tightened-up with a heavy "tug". Well hooked! I thought; and indeed he was. For the next ten minutes pandemonium ensued as the fish rushed up and down the pool, boring into the deep backwater on the far bank and up into the heavy stream in the neck. Eventually he dropped into the tail and after resting for a minute or two in quite shallow water, suddenly turned round and tore off downstream.

Fortunately my ghillie, Dougal MacDonnell, was with me. Forced into the rapids below the pool and wading through nearly half a mile of rocky river whose banks were lined with overhanging trees, I emerged at the head of the Long Pool where Dougal had been told to await me. I thought now that the fish would turn round, quieten down, and that we could gaff him in the pool. Not a bit of it! On he went, always seeming to swim downstream without ever turning. By now I was exhausted and decided to stop where I was, hold the fish as hard as I could and hope he did not break me. He did not. Instead, hard held, he swung quietly in towards the bank and lay still in the deep water alongside the bottom jetty in the Long

Pool where Dougal, who had left his gaff at the Dog Pool, lifted him out by the gills and with an arm round his belly threw this almost dead fish out onto the bank. He was hooked in the tail and, as a result of travelling so far "backwards" through such hard water had been practically drowned. As I looked at him I thought to myself, "here at last is a forty-pounder". Alas, he was only 38½ lbs!

Richard Waddington

An Excursion with the

March Brown

I have seen Thames trout chasing almost every species of fish who swim in the river, but I have never seen a trout, or a jack, after a perch. Folks say that the spikes worn by the perch make him an impossible meal and an unpalatable. But both trout and pike swallow their dinners head first and a perch's spines lie down when stroked head to tail. Yet both trout and pike take their quarry across the back in the first instance and, possibly, they have learned thus not to mell with anything so porcupine as a perch.

The loch trout in the North are hardier fellows – or hungrier. I must tell you of one of them. . . . I must tell my story for two reasons; one because I like to talk about big fish and another because a perch as the potential food of trout comes most apropos into it. So then: when I got out of the 2.25 from Waverley it was 3.45 or thereabouts and the sun of a wet summer was shining. Now I like going to places where I have never been before, especially if I find the sun there. And to be received by strangers as an old friend is pleasant too. And I like a chauffeur who loves his car, his employer, the country he lives in, and the art of angling – and who will talk about all these with enthusiasm the while he takes you 'where the sun and the wind are flying' and where tea is ready as soon as you are. I have heard the medically-minded inveigh against tea as a meal – especially the Scotch tea. But baps, fruit-gingerbread, jams and jeels, and all that go with them, remain my delight and my undoing. And now would I care to go down to the Loch? And the Loch that I am about to be free of is no popular resort, competitive and cosmopolitan. It is the resort, red-lettered, of the guests of its proprietor. These guests do not talk of their liberty overmuch lest they be deaved by their kin and acquaintance for a word to Himself. But if you mention a name in a tackle shop then, whether in Princes, Buchanan or any other street, the head of the firm will come out of the inner office and serve you personally.

At some time or other I imagine that the Loch was the labour of Mother Ice or else the crater of a volcano – if in Tweedside volcanoes were. Anyhow, there she is now, a mile of Loch maybe, and the pale, whale-backed bents that rise up from her, they slope gently to a pale sky. But do you, unbreathed, stroll up the eastward eminence you will get the surprise of your life. For, of a sudden, you will be standing a-top of five hundred foot of rock, and below you will be the sea crawling and rumbling in her terrible places down under, just to show you, this summer day, that she watches and she waits.

But you will spit upon her for luck, as I did (and just missed a rocketing blue-rock pigeon), and return to the Loch and be rowed out among the water-lilies in a miniature whale-boat. To fish most lochs is monotony, every cast the same cast and the maximum result of any one of them the possible pounder. But where your loch is a place of piscine milk and honey, a Canaan where a pounder becomes a five-pounder and a five-pounder – but, as of old they said, "we anticipate".

Anyhow, there is no monotony in loch fishing *this* August afternoon. What flies did I use? I can only remember that I fished three wet flies, little tiny ones, a-row. And that one of them was a March Brown. For the trout here are gentlemanly fellows who prefer a wee fly on light tackle to worm, wobbler, blue phantom or Silver Doctor, all of which, trusting to the good taste of his trout, the laird allows, even encourages. The afternoon was *lown*, here and there a dimple on the flat water, here and there a pucker. But never touch of a fish for me, and at seven I walked up the hill to dinner, encouraged by the notes of a pibroch blown, as "Neil himsel'" might have blown it, by amateur lungs. There was hare soup to eat with a potato in it; there was a three-pound trout for the pair of us, a notable *plat* and of a deeper pink and a nobler delicacy than are those of any salmon. There was a young grouse. There was a white wine, chilly to a charm, and a port to sit over. There was coffee strong as brandy and brandy soft as milk. I make these mercies my excuse for not being on the water again before nine.

The light was going and the air alive with bats. "I mind that one took my fly," said the keeper. "And what did you do with it?" "Oh, I just put it in my pocket and told my daughter (it's her that's parlourmaid) that she'd find a sweetie there – you'd have heard her scream here." "And what became of the bat?" "It wasna hurt and we just let it away again." Our boat drifts on. The glow of a cigar in the second boat waxes and wanes. "The moon is up and yet it is not night," and something close to the lily-beds takes me with a bang. He is among the stalks and out again, an acrobatic beggar, but presently the net is under him and, short and thick and golden and nearer three pounds than two, a trout is mine. And his twin brother joins him not ten minutes afterwards. And then, within a few casts, I get what the gods have been leading up to – a fish that takes resolutely and then goes headlong into deep water and "sounds" like a whale. A quarter of an hour later his weight is found to be five pounds and four ounces, and he is, I am told, the heaviest fish of the season – so far. And because of him I go home very happy and, full of the pride that apes humility, to bed.

Next morning, the laurels thick upon me, I am fishing by 10.30. A grey day it is, a cold day, a day of leaven waves and rocking lilies, a day of the *haar* that is blown in smoking squadrons. Likewise a day that wears to evening without a rise. An evening when a tired man might, and did, waver between port and sport, the ingle and the angle. But the angle had it. At 8.30 a pound trout repaid the angler and encouraged him to cast on and on and on . . .

It chapped ten o'clock and a sickly moon came struggling through. Near the landing stage the angler cast mechanically into shallow water. The trout that took the point fly went seventy yards before the rower could dip his oars and follow.

Now am I a peacock to display myself further? Why yes, of course I am, and only lack the words wherein to be loud speaking and lyrical. But I remember how, at long last, a great shape, symmetrical, thick, thickly dotted upon, and golden as honey, was in the net and a voice in the dark, a voice that sounded out of its ordnar', was speaking to me. "I've netted many a *salmon* that was smaller than this," it yammered.

This was a trout of eight pounds and eight ounces. And within him was a half-pound perch, spikes and all, and what he wanted with my wee March Brown I do not know.

from *At the Tail of the Weir*
by Patrick R. Chalmers, 1932.

MR THORNTON'S 50-POUNDERS

I have been the fortunate captor of two large salmon weighing 56 and 51 pounds respectively, and had an experience with another. Two fifty-pounders caught in the British Isles by one rod is, I believe, a record shared by myself, Professor Merton and the late Major A.W. Huntington.

Major Huntington and I both caught our fish in the River Awe, Argyll, and Professor Merton his in the River Wye. I shall now tell the tale of my first, a 56-pound fish.

The River Awe is a short river running out of Loch Awe and flowing into Loch Etive; it is a very strongly-flowing river, more than a very long cast across in many places; it is very rocky and when in spate, tears along with a lot of white water showing. Its banks are rough going in many places, and when a good fish tries to go out of a pool, there is no stopping him; he uses all his might in the strong water and fights downwards all the time.

In 1923 I began fishing on June 1st in good water conditions, and on the 4th had five salmon, 16 to 19 pounds, which is a very notable catch in the Awe. On the 6th a 42-pound fish took a 3/0 "Bulldog", a perfectly-shaped fish which was safely gaffed by Sam MacIntyre. I sent it off to Malloch to be set up, and it now adorns my bungalow on the Awe.

Better still was to come. On June 12th, after a rise in the water, I was fishing Pol Verie with a large "Green Highlander" in a drizzling rain, and near the tail of the pool I had a heavy dead pull, and nothing moved for a second or two, but when I lifted my rod (an 18-foot spliced Grant) and put some strain on, the fish moved out into the waves, and after a turn upwards he went off downstream, boring right out of the pool into the Little Verie. Out of that he ran down the rapids which were in spate, which meant a run at top speed with my rod held right up as high as possible to clear the rocks in that part. I had my line out beyond the backing, and the silk backing cutting into my fingers.

I had not yet seen the fish. He was dropping behind the rocks as he went down, but I steadied him in the Stone Pool, drawing him as much to my side of the river as possible. Presently he took up a position behind a big rock which had the main current running on the far side of it; it would have been "goodbye" if he went that way, so I held him very hard and worried him for an hour. As the strain increased he moved out and I pulled him back again, always keeping upstream above him, and his head pointed to the current; side-strain moved him away, so had to be immediately corrected to a straight pull. The fish came nearer me and, but for a rock jutting out, Sam might have gaffed him. Once his head came up.

Things were looking better and, drawing him to my side, I let him down some series of falls not far from me, but I had a cliff above me and some bad scrambling under trees, but I was pretty confident now I should get him in the Bothy Pool. I had been letting him drop from fall to fall with a light strain on, so when he came to the Bothy he was still strong, and went right out into the heavy stream and out of the pool.

This had been difficult going for some time, but now I came to a grass track with no need to hurry, so I started swinging him to the side and going through the Three Ash Pools. I pulled him to my side, still upright in the water and, in a small quiet bay, drew him inwards. Sam, leaning over a rock, had a good chance to gaff him square, as his head rested between two small rocks. I caught Sam (aged nearly seventy) by the coat, so that he shouldn't fall in, and out he lifted the best fish of my life! A great fight lasting two and a half hours, and ending five hundred yards from where he was hooked. I took him into Taynuilt to be weighed roughly, and sent him off to Malloch of Perth to be set up, who made him 56 pounds the next day; the measurements were 52 inches long, 29 girth.

Mr Hutton said two years in the river and four years feeding in the sea.

Two ladies who were looking on from the opposite bank all this time and had brought me luck, drove me to Taynuilt, and I took back a bottle of Giesler to celebrate!

Next day I lent my beat to a friend because I was so stiff in the shoulders. I recommend a long gaff on the Awe; here had been the chance for its use that might have ended the fight half-an-hour sooner. The power of a heavy salmon with the Awe in spate has to be experienced to be believed. It is a notorious river for the fighting powers of its fish, two out of three hooked and out on the bank is good going. Awe fish are short, thick, and small-headed, and this one was fresh run from the sea about three miles away.

After renting the Breadalbane water on the Awe for nine years, the proprietor wanted more rent, so I gave it up and fished at Soval, Isle of Lewis, which is my property. But always I was thinking of the big fish in the Awe, and of my long rods which had lain idle for three years. I heard my Awe beat was for sale, so, after quick negotiations I secured it, with a very little land and the keeper's house. This was very thrilling for me!

I started on April 24, 1934, earlier than was my usual custom, and got out my rod. Johnny MacIntyre, the Bonawe keeper, had an 18-pound fish, the first of the season in the Disputed, and next day I got one in the same pool on a Silver Devon, a proper beauty of 32 pounds. This was a nice start for my new ownership.

A day or two later I was fishing a prawn with my 18-foot Castle Connel; the water was very heavy and I got nothing, but fancied I had a light touch in the Seal Pool. Next morning I tried Pol Verie, which proved a blank, and then moved up to the Seal, about 150 yards above. Coming near the tail of it I had a hard pull at the spot exactly where I had had an indication on the previous day.

There was no mistake this time. I was into a heavy fish and I moved to the good going on the bank above, worked him to the head of the pool, and then to the tail again, and so on for some twenty minutes, everything going excellently and some heavy strain put in, but presently he had enough of that, and bolted out into the centre of the river, making for Pol Nugan rocks. However, my ideas were different, and I swung him across to my side where, with a long gaff, John Jack my ghillie, might have had a chance: but the going there was bad, and Jack nearly took a bath. I called him out and let my fish down the falls, I going all out, full speed down the bank beside the long Verie falls, up a steep path onto the road above and, holding up now quite easily above him, I steered him down the falls and then stood fast; with a heavy strain on, I brought him to my side in quieter water, plunging and splashing. Here I towed him towards the gaff which Jack got well home, and my fish was on the bank. I knew I had a whopper, but he was heavier than I thought, as he bumped down my 50-pound scales; and when I took him to the village and station I found he weighed 51 pounds.

This was beyond what I ever expected to do with big fish. It was eleven years since I had had the 56-pounder. I have a photograph of him, but no more setting up in a glass case! He measured 50 inches long and 27½ girth – hooked at 11.30 and killed at 12.10, quite quick time for a big fish.

These two big fish and a big fast-flowing river, full of rocks, in grand scenery gave one the very highest one can expect in salmon-fishing. Some people may ask if I have had other big fish on, or risen. Well, it is difficult to say. I have killed several 40-pound fish, and can remember one or two big ones. There was a great wild fish that ran out almost as soon as he was hooked – down Pol Verie, out of Little Verie, down the rapids to the Stone Pool, never stopping, he ran to the far side from me right away till 150 yards of line was all gone, the gut went pop, and my large "Mar Lodge" was gone with him!

Sam MacIntyre was with me when a huge one sailed out after the fly in the Disputed Pool, a place where one can see well. He stopped just short of the fly, as the water was getting shallower. Sam said he must have been 60 pounds, and he certainly was enormous. I never saw him again.

I also rose one in Pol Verie, near the stepping-stones, which left quite a hollow in the water as though a boat was going down. I used to boast that no fish would take me an hour to kill. But I know better now.

It was on June 11, 1937, the year in which I became sixty-eight, that I was fishing the Awe again. I had been getting some sport and things were going well, so, full of confidence, I went up to the Shallows (which is at the top of my beat, just below the Brander Burn) at ten o'clock. I started with 5/5 gut that I had been using recently, and stepped out onto the pier and began fishing. Almost immediately, just below me, I was into a fish which splashed on the surface; I said to my young ghillie, Jim Jack, "That's a monster". He soon rushed right across the river almost to the far bank. I got him at once, reeling like mad, and he came back to where I had hooked him, and not far from me, playing up and down the pool; in that part a proper dog-fight took place, and I fairly hustled him, but he did not show again. I was here a long time, and a crowd of cars and people collected to look on, as it was close to the road. I was thinking that 5/5 gut was not going to stand the strain, and I knew that I was at a big disadvantage; it would require hands and experience to get this fish in, and a lot of luck on top of that.

After a time he moved out and down, and presently descended the rapids, so I had to get moving quickly, though the crowd was a good deal in my way. He stopped in the falls behind a rock, and I ought to have been content to stay there, but side-strained him instead, and off he went to the Black Pool, a hundred yards below. I kept a strong lift on him, and I could see his length and size, as he was in about three feet of water. Here, in the light of after events, I made a mistake. I should have stuck it out as long as I could there, and possibly the ghillie might have had a snatch at him with the gaff. One must remember the river was in spate, and once out of the pool there was no stopping until the next large one was reached. However, I am convinced this was the turning-point of the day. I moved him, and away he went to the Seal Pool, where he was steadier, but not for very long; out he went to try for Pol Nugan. I swung him across to my side, and he sank below a big rock not very far out. I kept a heavy strain on to tire him before he went down the Verie rapids, which was going to mean a long run for me at full speed to keep up and over him. He stuck it for some time, but then he came out and down the falls at a maximum pace, and I arrived at Pol Verie still feeling I might have him here. I rolled him over about three feet of water, and saw all his white belly, after which he followed steadily, with me walking him up, but there were no signs of his failing, and the way he fought here made me say to one onlooker, "He seems as fresh as ever". Presently out he went down the rapids to the Stone Pool. Here I used the same tactics as with my 56-pound fish, which proved effective. I did just see his head lift out of the water before he went down the falls under the cliff. People in their excitement pushed me over the bad places and somehow I got to the Bothy Pool with my fish still on and going strong. I had hopes here, but not good ones, of a finish; the water was too strong for me, and we fought it out down to the three Ash Tree Pools. There I got on terms with him, drawing him almost to my bank, but he must have seen the people above or a yellow jumper or something which scared him, and he sailed out again. I had taken a breather and managed to get my line freshly wound on, as it had been loose and overlapping, and a strong run might have caused a hitch.

Down past the Colonel's and Spring Pools at full speed I was taken, over a wall at the bottom of the falls to where there was a sort of basin, at the outside of which the fish showed; he came almost to a gaffing chance if anyone had been there, and then he sank. About this time I got cramp in my right arm from so much reeling and watching the water from ten o'clock till about two-thirty made things a bit dizzy. I sat on a rock on the edge of the river and took a rest, a friend meanwhile holding the fish with a steady strain on. Presently I took the rod and tried to end matters, but my fish dropped down in very fast water, and nothing would make him come to the side. I felt sure he was really done now; he kept sinking and letting the current help him; this went on for a long time, until he was getting near some trees overhanging the river above the Meal Pool. The end was coming, I knew, but getting my friend again to hold the rod with a strain on, I got out to review the position on the bank.

It was very bad, but I thought if he kept out in the middle of the river we might get along, in and out, with help. With a last great effort to drag him to the side I had to let him go. He came then to the bushes, hanging in the water there, and after passing the rod from man to man, we came to a clearing, and I took the rod but the line was slack. He had gone.

The time was now three-fifteen, five and a quarter hours after hooking him. I have thought since I might have tried hand-lining him at the basin above, but it should be remembered that 5/5 would hardly stand that. Pulling him from below would have been useless. There was no chance of sending him up, there was no slack water to which to send him, the river was in such a rush. The company I had in the morning were still with me, but I shall always think, that if I had been by myself with a very experienced ghillie, that fish would have been killed. I put him at nearer 60 pounds than 50. He may have been hooked outside the jaw, but it was certainly in the head, as I pulled it up once.

That was that! I retired, wet through, back to tea, having only had a cold water drink since the morning, and come a mile down the river through ten pools. At about half-time my daughter had said, "Would you like a drink?" as I passed my bungalow, and I agreed it would be a help. She brought me a glass of water. God knows why!

After a change and some tea, I went up to my morning starting-place and got a 17-pound fish. I said to him, "You can't *all* treat the old man like the big one did." Perhaps some day I will catch another monster . . . But no. I have had all the luck that can come to one fisherman, and now I have put in three-score years and ten, the odds will be too heavy. Two out of three hooked and on the bank in the Awe is good work, so I leave it at that, and as my gallery of friends of that day said at the end – "It was a good show" – then that must be my consolation!

H.G. Thornton, from *Game and Gun
and Angler's Monthly*, April, 1940

A Big Spey Salmon

When I had my lucky chance, I had only caught a few salmon, all those on a fly; my casting was still terrible. Unexpectedly, I was asked to go and fish on the Spey, with my cousin Jim who had taken the Delagyle boat at Aberlour. At the last moment, one of the experienced rods could not go. I nervously and excitedly accepted, knowing the other rods were very experienced fishermen. I had only fished on smaller northern Scottish rivers and felt daunted at the thought of the size and fame of the Spey.

My plane was delayed and very late. I was sleepy and agitated when I saw the swollen river rushing past me. My rod looked inadequate and so did my fly box, which I had sat on and broken on the plane. We were told that in these conditions spinning was our best chance. In those days I did what I was told, and as I had only ever spun off a pier, I knew that a few yards was probably as far as I should be able to "chuck and chance". The other rods seemed to know where to fish. I walked up the river to a boarded bend, a deep pool, feeling rather hopeless. I did not realise in those days that in such high and strong water the salmon would probably be near and under the bank so I was very surprised and relieved to see a fish head and tail only a few feet into the river. What luck, I thought, as I knew I could easily cast that far. I moved away very quietly and went back to the fishing hut, collected my rod and tied on a yellow and green Devon. Why that one, I don't know. It was the first time I had ever tied anything on to my spinning-rod myself. Nervously I showed the knot to Jimmy, who said, "Yes, that will do", and off I went back to the corner, excited and full of hope.

Keeping well away from the bank, I had several casts to where I had seen the fish. About the sixth cast, all in the same place, I suddenly felt a huge tug, and the line went taut. I didn't know then that big fish often seem to sit on the bottom for a while. I called to Jimmy and he said, "Sure you're not on the bottom?" Before I could answer, the fish moved, very slowly but very powerfully. He moved upstream, pulling me along with him. I was so worried about my knot, that I decided my only hope was to play him very carefully, as I felt my knot would break at any moment. After some time the ghillie came near to me and suggested I play the fish harder, as I seemed to be taking so long. I told him I was nervous about my bad knot. In my total ignorance I did the right thing for the wrong reasons. The fish literally pulled me very slowly upstream with a steady pull, never showing. If this ever happened to me now, I think I should be in such a state of shock and excitement that I should probably lose the fish. One hour later, the fish had reached a pool before a long shallower run. I was again advised to be harder on the fish. I pretended not to hear. I was not only thinking of the knot; I believe it is also a woman's intuition to be careful. Suddenly the fish showed itself and then rolled. I could not believe my eyes: it looked enormous. I did not know what to do so I did nothing, just tried to keep my rod up. He rolled about in the pool in a frightening way. Was it really a salmon after all? Suddenly he seemed to give up. Jimmy and the ghillie appeared with the net, surprised, I am sure, that I still had it on. I reeled-in very carefully, dragging it through the water. How amazed we were at the size – not all of him could be got into the net. How happy I was that I had two experienced netters. The fish weighed 45 lb 6 oz and really was a salmon! It proves to me, no matter what men say, that women should follow their own intuitions.

Lilla Rowcliffe

BY THE SKIN OF HIS TEETH

In the month of July, some thirty years ago, one Duncan Grant, a shoemaker by profession, who was more addicted to fishing than to his craft, went up the way from the village of Aberlour, in the north, to take a cast in some of the pools above Elchies Water. He had no great choice of tackle, as may be conceived; nothing, in fact, but what was useful, and scant supply of that.

Duncan tried one or two pools without success, till he arrived at a very deep and rapid stream, facetiously termed "the Mountebank": here he paused, as if meditating whether he should throw his line or not. "She is very big," said he to himself, "but I'll try her; if I grip him he'll be worth the hauding." He then fished it, a step and a throw, about half-way down, when a heavy splash proclaimed that he had raised him, though he missed the fly. Going back a few paces, he came over him again, and hooked him. The first tug verified to Duncan his prognostication, that if he was there "he would be worth the hauding"; but his tackle had thirty plies of hair next the fly, and he held fast, nothing daunted. Give and take went on with dubious advantage, the fish occasionally sulking. The thing at length became serious; and, after a succession of the same tactics, Duncan found himself at the Boat of Aberlour, seven hours after he had hooked his fish, the said fish fast under a stone, and himself completely tired. He had some thoughts of breaking his tackle and giving the thing up; but he finally hit

58

upon an expedient to rest himself, and at the same time to guard against the surprise and consequence of a sudden movement of the fish. He laid himself down comfortably on the banks, the butt end of his rod in front; and most ingeniously drew out part of his line, which he held in his teeth. "If he tugs when I'm sleeping," said he, "I think I'll find him noo"; and no doubt it is probable that he would. Accordingly, after a comfortable nap of three or four hours, Duncan was awoke by a most unceremonious tug at his jaws. In a moment he was on his feet, his rod well up, and the fish swattering down the stream. He followed as best he could, and was beginning to think of the rock at Craigellachie, when he found to his great relief that he could "get a pull on him". He had now comparatively easy work; and exactly twelve hours after hooking him, he cleicked him at the head of Lord Fife's water: he weighed fifty-four pounds, Dutch, and had the tide lice upon him.

from *Days and Nights of Salmon Fishing*
by William Scrope, 1843

INDIA

No Flies on Jim

During a pause in his quest to kill a man-eating leopard in the hills of India, Jim Corbett went fishing.

I was returning one day towards the latter end of March, after visiting a village on the Kedarnath pilgrim route, when, as I approached a spot where the road runs close alongside the Mandakini river, and where there is a waterfall ten to twelve feet high, I saw a number of men sitting on the rock at the head of the fall on the far side of the river, armed with a triangular net attached to a long bamboo pole. The roar of the water prevented conversation, so leaving the road I sat down on the rocks on my side of the fall, to have a rest and a smoke – for I had walked far that day – and to see what the men were doing.

Presently one of the men got to his feet, and as he pointed down excitedly into the foaming white water at the foot of the fall, two of his companions manning the long pole held the triangular net close to the fall. A large shoal of mahseer fish, varying in size from five to fifty pounds, were attempting to leap the fall. One of these fish, about ten pounds in weight, leapt clear of the fall and when falling back was expertly caught in the net. After the fish had been extracted and placed in a basket, the net was again held out close to the fall. I watched the sport for about an hour, during which time the men caught four fish, all about the same size – ten pounds.

On my previous visit to Rudraprayag I had been informed by the chowkidar in charge of the Inspection Bungalow that there was good fishing in the spring – before the snow-water came down – in both the Alaknanda and Mandakini rivers, so I had come armed on this my second visit with a fourteen-foot split cane salmon rod, a Silex reel with two hundred and fifty yards of line, a few stout traces, and an assortment of home-made brass spoons varying in size from one to two inches.

The following morning – as no news had come in of the man-eater – I set off for the waterfall with my rod and tackle.

No fish were leaping the fall as they had been doing the previous day, and the men on the far side of the river were sitting in a group round a small fire smoking a hookah which was passing from hand to hand. They watched me with interest.

Below the waterfall was a pool thirty to forty yards wide, flanked on both sides by a wall of rock, and about two hundred yards long, one hundred yards of which was visible from where I stood at the head of the pool. The water in this beautiful and imposing pool was crystal-clear.

The rock face at the head of the pool rose sheer up out of the water to a height of twelve feet, and after keeping at this height for twenty yards, sloped gradually upwards to a height of a hundred feet. It was not possible to get down to water level anywhere on my side of the pool, nor would it be possible, or profitable, to follow a fish – assuming that I hooked one – along the bank, for at the top of the high ground there were trees and bushes, and at the tail of the pool the river cascaded down in a foaming torrent to its junction with the Alaknanda. To land a fish in this pool would be a difficult and a hazardous task, but the crossing of that bridge could be deferred until the fish had been hooked – and I had not yet put together my rod.

On my side of the pool the water – shot through with millions of small bubbles – was deep, and from about halfway across a shingle bottom was showing, over which four to six feet of water was flowing. Above this shingle bottom, every stone and pebble of which was visible in the clear water, a number of fish, ranging in size from three to ten pounds, were slowly moving upstream.

As I watched these fish, standing on the rocks twelve feet above the water with a two-inch spoon mounted with a single strong treble hook in my hand, a flight of fingerlings flashed out of the deep water and went skimming over the shingle bottom, hotly pursued by three big mahseer. Using the good salmon rod as friend Hardy had never intended that it should be used – and as it had been used on many previous occasions – I slung the spoon out, and in my eagerness over-estimated the distance, with the result that the spoon struck the rock on the far side of the pool, about two feet above the water. The falling of the spoon into the water coincided with the arrival of the fingerlings at the rock, and the spoon had hardly touched the water, when it was taken by the leading mahseer.

Striking with a long line from an elevated position entails a very heavy strain, but my good rod stood the strain, and the strong treble hook was firmly fixed in the mahseer's mouth. For a moment or two the fish did not appear to realize what had happened as, standing perpendicularly in the water with his white belly towards me, he shook his head from side to side, and then, possibly frightened by the dangling spoon striking against his head, he gave a mighty splash and went tearing downstream, scattering in all directions the smaller fish that were lying on the shingle bottom.

In his first run the mahseer ripped a hundred yards of line off the reel, and after a moment's check carried on for another fifty yards. There was plenty of line still on the reel, but the fish had now gone round the bend and was getting dangerously near the tail of the pool. Alternately easing and tightening the strain on the line, I eventually succeeded in turning his head upstream, and having done so, very gently pulled him round the bend, into the hundred yards of water I was overlooking.

Just below me a projection of rock had formed a backwater, and into this backwater the fish, after half an hour's game fight, permitted himself to be drawn.

I had now very definitely reached my bridge and had just regretfully decided that, as there was no way of crossing it, the fish would have to be cut adrift, when a shadow fell across the rock beside me. Peering over the rock into the backwater, the new arrival remarked that it was a very big fish, and in the same breath asked what I was going to do about it. When I told him that it would not be possible to draw the fish up the face of the rock, and that therefore the only thing to do was to cut it free, he said, 'Wait, sahib, I will fetch my brother'. His brother – a long and lanky stripling with dancing eyes – had quite evidently

65

been cleaning out a cowshed when summoned, so telling him to go upstream and wash himself lest he should slip on the smooth rock, I held council with the elder man.

Starting from where we were standing, a crack, a few inches wide, ran irregularly down the face of the rock, ending a foot above the water in a ledge some six inches wide. The plan we finally agreed on was that the stripling – who presently returned with his arms and legs glistening with water – should go down to the ledge, while the elder brother went down the crack far enough to get hold of the stripling's left hand, while I lay on the rock holding the elder brother's other hand. Before embarking on the plan I asked the brothers whether they knew how to handle a fish and whether they could swim, and received the laughing answer that they had handled fish and swum in the river from childhood.

The snag in the plan was that I could not hold the rod and at the same time make a link in the chain. However, some risk had to be taken, so I put the rod down and held the line in my hand, and when the brothers had taken up position I sprawled on the rock and, reaching down, got hold of the elder brother's hand. Then very gently I drew the fish towards the rock, holding the line alternately with my left hand and with my teeth. There was no question that the stripling knew how to handle a fish, for before the fish had touched the rock, he had inserted his thumb into one side of the gills and his fingers into the other, getting a firm grip on the fish's throat. Up to this point the fish had been quite amenable, but on having its throat seized, it lashed out, and for seconds it appeared that the three of us would go headlong into the river.

Both brothers were barefooted, and when I had been relieved of the necessity of holding the line and was able to help with both hands, they turned and, facing the rock, worked their way up with their toes, while I pulled lustily from on top.

When the fish at last had been safely landed, I asked the brothers if they ate fish, and on receiving their eager answer that they most certainly did, when they could get any, I told them I would give them the fish we had just landed – a mahseer in grand condition weighing a little over thirty pounds – if they would help me to land another fish for my men. To this they very readily agreed.

The treble had bitten deep into the leathery underlip of the mahseer, and as I cut it out, the brothers watched interestedly. When the hook was free, they asked if they might have a look at it. Three hooks in one, such a thing had never been seen in their village. The bit of bent brass of course acted as a sinker. With what were the hooks baited? Why should fish want to eat brass? And was it really brass, or some kind of hardened bait? When the spoon, and the trace with its three swivels, had been commented on and marvelled at, I made the brothers sit down and watch while I set about catching the second fish.

The biggest fish in the pool were at the foot of the fall, but here in the foaming white water, in addition to mahseer were some very big goonch, a fish that takes a spoon or dead bait very readily, and which is responsible for 90 per cent of the tackle lost in our hill rivers through its annoying habit of diving to the bottom of the pool when hooked and getting its head under a rock from where it is always difficult, and often impossible, to dislodge it.

No better spot than the place from where I had made my first cast was available, so here I again took up my position, with rod in hand and spoon held ready for casting.

The fish on the shingle bottom had been disturbed while I was playing the mahseer and by our subsequent movements on the face of the rock but were now beginning to return, and presently an exclamation from the brothers, and an excited pointing of fingers, drew my attention to a big fish downstream where the shingle bottom ended and the deep water began. Before I was able to make a cast, the fish turned and disappeared in the deep water, but a little later it reappeared, and as it came into the shallow water I made a cast, but owing to the line being wet the cast fell short. The second cast was beautifully placed and beautifully timed, the spoon striking the water exactly where I wanted it to. Waiting for a second to give the spoon time to sink, I started to wind in the line, giving the spoon just the right amount of spin, and as I drew it along in little jerks, the mahseer shot forward, and next moment, with the hook firmly fixed in his mouth, jumped clean out of the water, fell back with a great splash, and went madly downstream, much to the excitement of the spectators, for the men on the far bank had been watching the proceedings as intently as the brothers.

As the reel spun round and the line paid out, the brothers – now standing one on either side of me – urged me not to let the fish go down the run at the tail of the pool. Easier said than done, for it is not possible to stop the first mad rush of a mahseer of any size without risking certain break, or the tearing away of the hook-hold. Our luck was in, or else the fish feared the run, for when there was less than fifty yards of line on the reel he checked, and though he continued to fight gamely he was eventually drawn round the bend, and into the little backwater at the foot of the rock.

The landing of this second fish was not as difficult as the landing of the first had been, for we each knew our places on the rock and exactly what to do.

Both fish were the same length, but the second was a little heavier than the first, and while the elder brother set off in triumph for his village with his fish carried over his shoulder – threaded on a grass cable he had made – the stripling begged to be allowed to accompany me back to the Inspection Bungalow, and to carry both my fish and my rod. Having in the days of long ago been a boy myself, and having had a brother who fished, there was no need for the stripling when making his request to have said, "If you will let me carry both the fish and the rod, and will walk a little distance behind me, sahib, all the people who see me on the road, and in the bazaar, will think that I have caught this great fish, the like of which they have never seen."

from *The Man-Eating Leopard of Rudraprayag*,
by Jim Corbett

DINNER IN THE FIELD

"A" and "K" are mahseer fishing in N. India, March 1867.
This is "K's" account

Though, for some mysterious reason, I never had good sport in the early morning fishing, still I was up again next morning by sunrise, and we both tried the pool from the boat; I literally did nothing – did not even stir a fish; but A. landed one of 19 lbs. At 3 pm I went up the river and fished the head of a small pool, with a glorious stream running into it, close by some jutting rocks. Here I landed a 4-pounder and a 22-pounder with phantom and spoon. I then tried a stream a little higher up. I suspect the water was rather too heavy – at least, I stirred nothing; so having given the lower stream an hour's rest, I returned to it, and put on a natural bait. I soon hooked and landed one of 14 lbs, when I put on a fresh bait, intending to have a few more casts before it got dark, it being then a quarter to six, and rather cloudy. The bait had just come across the stream and was entering the backwater, when I felt a vigorous tug, and a monster rushed off down stream, with nearly 100 yards of line before I managed to stop him. Then he tried a run up stream to nearly opposite where I was standing, then down again, then opposite me again, but on quite the further side of the river, and there he sulked for the best part of an hour, all of which time I was keeping a very severe pull on him.

Unfortunately, I was fishing from a point of rock, and on my left hand, down stream, was what is best described as "a long bay" of dead water, 50 yards or so across, and between it and the stream was a bar, consisting of huge rocks rising to within 2 feet or 3 feet of the surface, but with intervals varying from 2 feet to 6 feet between them, so that getting below the fish was quite out of the question. At last I managed to move him, and he dashed down stream 70 or 80 yards, and sulked there. Now commenced my task. I soon found that merely keeping a steady pull on him had no effect, especially as he was now below me. The pressure I kept on him was so great that attempting to wind up line simply caused the line to sink between the coils already on the reel; so my only plan was to draw in an inch or so of the line with my hand, and then wind it up on the reel. By dint of perseverance I succeeded in getting him up to within 20 yards or so, and then not another inch could I gain; but I managed to rile him apparently, for off he rushed to the bottom of the stream again. Of course by this time it was pitch dark, or else I should have been tempted to try and effect a passage across the bar, with the almost certainty of going in over head and ears. As it was, prudence carried the day, and I sat down on a rock, put the butt of my rod between my legs, and lit a pipe. I then sent my fisherman off to camp, about two and a quarter miles over very rough ground, to order some dinner to be brought out, besides dry shoes and socks, and a great-coat. By the time the welcome sight of a lantern appeared it was near ten o'clock, and all the time I had been fighting for every inch of line. There was a splice in my line, and the struggle I had to get it on the reel is almost incredible. Time after time I felt it pass through my fingers and just reach the reel, when the fish would shake his head, and pull it half-way down the rod again.

After some little delay in collecting sticks and lighting the fire, I managed to make a very tolerable meal, keeping a tight hold on the line with one hand while I used the other for dinner purposes. Feeling much refreshed by my hasty repast, I devoted all my energies to my enemy with redoubled ardour. After one or two runs, I fancied there appeared to be something wrong with the reel, so, calling for a light, I examined it, and found to my discomfort that the two screws which connect the reel with the bar that was tied on to the rod were gone, and, of course, on the same side as the handle; the consequence was that the mere act of winding up caused the reel to gape very considerably at this opening. I tried various methods for remedying this mishap, such as getting my fisherman to hold it as firmly as possible in his hands while I wound up line, etc; but I found none of them so satisfactory as crossing my legs as I sat on the rock, and pressing the reel against my left knee. This answered tolerably well, but it was a somewhat awkward position to remain in for long. To make a long story short, however, about 2 a.m. I prevailed on my fish to cross the bar and have a swim in the deep, still pool. He gave two furious runs up and down, I luckily just preventing him from returning to the stream, and then I hauled him into a nice little shallow creek. The fisherman carefully handled him, and he was secured. I made my man carry the captive some yards from the water, and deposit him in a safe place, and then a most pleasant sensation of triumph filled my heart, as by the light of the lantern I gloated over the splendid fish which had fought so bravely and pluckily for eight hours and a half. By this time it was 2.30 a.m., so my servants shouldered the fish, pots and pans, and we started off home, floundering about over the two miles and a half of boulders and shingle in pitch darkness, as the lantern had burned out. On arrival I, of course, routed up A., and we weighed the fish. He just turned the scale at 52 lbs, and was 4 feet 5 inches in length, which I must confess rather disappointed me, as I had landed in the previous year one of 57 lbs that had not given anything like the sport of this one.

from *The Field*
October 1869

How to Catch a Crocodile

Crocodiles are very shy, and not to be caught, except by night line. A simple way of setting this is to get a bamboo of full thickness, and 10 or 22 feet in length. To one end of it tie a hook with only a foot of line between hook and bamboo. I used three large sea hooks tied together like a treble hook. The line should not be a single cord, which the crocodile can bite in two, but fifteen or twenty pieces of common twine tied together at the ends, but not twisted at all. These will get between his teeth, and escape being bitten, and their united strength will hold him fast enough. Bait the hook, which must be a large and very strong one, with a bull frog, or a fowl's entrails, or a couple of crows, or any meat, and push the whole out into the lake, pool, or fort moat in which the crocodiles are, and leave it for the night. If there is a slight current, it is easy enough to attach a stone, by way of anchor, by a long string to the other end of the bamboo, and to drop it in. The line between the bamboo and the hook being so short, the bait is kept near the surface, and is not liable to be concealed amongst weeds, etc., at the bottom; when the crocodile takes the bait and turns down with it, the shortness of the line, and the ready opposition of the floating bamboo, quickly strikes the hook into him, and the more he tries to get down the more stoutly the bamboo resists him, for it is full of air from end to end, and is a very powerful buoy. As long as he keeps to the water the bamboo plays him well, and if he tries the land he will soon be brought up with a round turn by the bamboo getting hitched amongst bushes. As far as my experience goes they always take to the land eventually.

I have been told that good fun can be had out of the crocodile by baiting as above in the daytime, and setting a man to watch from a distance in concealment. The man must be very still, and well concealed, and at a distance, or not a crocodile will be hooked, for they are very wary. Directly one is hooked he gives the information. Then into small boats quick, one man in each prow with a hog spear, start fair, and "ride" or "off" for first spear. As he sees the boats coming, down goes the crocodile, and up stands the bamboo, more and more upright the deeper he goes, so that the more he tries to avoid you the more conspicuous becomes his course. Follow him up, for if the bamboo is a big one, as it should be, it will be so strongly buoyant that he must come to the top soon. There, now, the bamboo is beginning to slope, showing that he is coming to the surface. Now is your time for a spear. But look out for his tail – it is very powerful. If he upsets you, he has big brothers about, and they may reverse the sport.

The Rod in India
H.S. Thomas, 3rd ed. 1897

OCCASIONAL HAZARDS

An objection to wading is said to be that you are now and then swallowed by a crocodile. But I have not experienced that sensation yet, and though there are crocodiles enough, I do not think there is really anything to be feared from them. I have again and again waded in just where I have seen a crocodile disappear, or have noticed fresh footmarks and basking places.

An acquaintance of mine was stripping for a swim in a tempting-looking pool, his native attendant silently watching him all unconcerned till he eventually dropped the casual remark: "There are about thirty of them in that pool" "Thirty what?" asked the white man. "Crocodiles," was the still unconcerned reply. The undressing for a swim in that pool was promptly discontinued.

H.S. Thomas
The Rod in India 3rd ed. 1897

THE FISH OF MY DREAMS

Fishing for mahseer in a well-stocked submontane river is, in my opinion, the most fascinating of all field sports. Our environments, even though we may not be continuously conscious of them, nevertheless play a very important part in the sum total of our enjoyment of any form of outdoor sport. I am convinced that the killing of the fish of one's dreams in uncongenial surroundings would afford an angler as little pleasure as the winning of the Davis Cup would to a tennis player if the contest were staged in the Sahara.

The river I have recently been fishing in flows, for some forty miles of its length, through a beautifully wooded valley, well stocked with game and teeming with bird life. I had the curiosity to count the various kinds of animals and birds seen in one day, and by the evening of that day my count showed, among animals, sambur, chital, kakar, ghooral, pig, langur and red monkeys; and among birds seventy-five varieties including peafowl, red jungle fowl, kaleege pheasants, black partridge and bush quail.

In addition to these I saw a school of five otter in the river, several small mugger and a python. The python was lying on the surface of a big still pool, with only the top of its flat head and eyes projecting above the gin-clear water. The subject was one I had long wished to photograph, and in order to do this it was necessary to cross the river above the pool and climb the opposite hillside; but unfortunately I had been seen by those projecting eyes, and as I cautiously stepped backwards, the reptile, which appeared to be about eighteen feet long, submerged, to retire to its subterranean home among the piled-up boulders at the head of the pool.

In some places the valley through which the river flows is so narrow that a stone can be tossed with ease from one side to the other, and in other places it widens out to a mile or more. In these open spaces grow amaltas with their two-feet-long sprays of golden bloom, Karaunda and box bushes with their white star-shaped flowers. The combined scent from these flowers fills the air, throbbing with the spring songs of a multitude of birds, with the most delicate and pleasing of perfumes. In these surroundings angling for mahseer might well be described as sport fit for kings. My object in visiting this sportsman's paradise was not, however, to kill mahseer, but to try to secure a daylight picture of a tiger, and it was only when light conditions were unfavourable that I laid aside my movie camera for a rod.

I had been out from dawn one day, trying, hour after hour, to get a picture of a tigress and her two cubs. The tigress was a young animal, nervous as all young mothers are, and as often as I stalked her she retired with the cubs into heavy cover. There is a limit to the disturbance a tigress, be she young or old, will suffer when accompanied by cubs, and when the limit on this occasion had been reached I altered my tactics and tried sitting up in trees over open glades, and lying in high grass near a stagnant pool in which she and her family were accustomed to drink, but with no better success.

When the declining sun was beginning to cast shadows over the open places I was watching, I gave up the attempt, and added the day to the several hundred days I had already spent in trying to get a picture of a tiger in its natural surroundings. The two men I had brought from camp had passed the day in the shade of a tree on the far side of the river. I instructed them to return to camp by way of the forest track, and, exchanging my camera for a rod, set off along the river, intent on catching a fish for my dinner.

The fashion in rods and tackle has altered, in recent years, as much as the fashion in ladies' dresses. Gone, one often wonders where, are the 18-foot greenheart rods with their unbreakable accompaniments, and gone the muscles to wield them, and their place has been taken by light one-handed fly rods.

I was armed with an ll-foot tournament trout rod, a reel containing 50 yards of casting line and 200 yards of fine silk backing, a medium gut cast, and a one-inch home-made brass spoon.

When one has unlimited undisturbed water to fish one is apt to be over-critical. A pool is discarded because the approach to it is over rough ground, or a run is rejected because of a suspected snag. On this occasion, half a mile had been traversed before a final selection was made: a welter of white water cascading over rocks at the head of a deep oily run 80 yards long, and at the end of the run a deep still pool 200 yards long and 70 yards wide. Here was the place to catch the fish for my dinner.

Standing just clear of the white water I flicked the spoon into the run, pulling a few yards of line off the reel as I did so, and as I raised the rod to allow the line to run through the rings the spoon was taken by a fish, near the bank, and close to where I was standing. By great good luck the remaining portion of the slack line tightened on the drum of the reel and did not foul the butt of the rod or handle of the reel, as so often happens.

In a flash the fish was off downstream, the good well-oiled reel singing a paean of joy as the line was stripped off it. The 50 yards of casting line followed by 100 yards of backing were gone, leaving in their passage burned furrows in the fingers of my left hand, when all at once the mad rush ceased as abruptly as it had begun, and the line went dead.

The speculations one makes on these occasions chased each other through my mind, accompanied by a little strong language to ease my feelings. The hold had been good without question. The cast, made up a few days previously from short lengths of gut procured from the Pilot Gut Coy., had been carefully tied and tested. Suspicion centred on the split ring; possibly, cracked on a stone on some previous occasion, it had now given way.

Sixty yards of the line are back on the reel, when the slack line is seen to curve to the left, and a moment later is cutting a strong furrow upstream – the fish is still on, and is heading for the white water. Established here, pulling alternately from upstream, at right angles, and downstream fails to dislodge him. Time drags on, and the conviction grows that the fish has gone, leaving the line hung up on a snag. Once again and just as hope is being abandoned the line goes slack, and then tightens a moment later, as the fish for the second time goes madly downstream.

And now he appears to have made up his mind to leave this reach of the river for the rapids below the pool. In one strong steady run he reaches the tail of the pool. Here, where the water fans out and shallows, he hesitates, and finally returns to the pool. A little later he shows on the surface for the first time, and but for the fact that the taut line runs direct from the point of the rod to the indistinctly seen object on the far side of the pool, it would be impossible to believe that the owner of that great triangular fin, projecting five inches out of the water, had taken a fly spoon a yard or two from my feet.

Back in the depths of the pool, he was drawn inch by inch into slack water. To land a big fish single-handed on a trout rod is not an easy accomplishment. Four times he was stranded with a portion of his great shoulders out of water, and four times at my very cautious approach he lashed out, and, returning to the pool, had to be fought back inch by inch. At the fifth attempt, with the butt of the rod held at the crook of my thumb and reversed, rings upwards to avoid the handle of the reel coming into contact with him, he permits me to place one hand and then the other against his sides and very gently propel him through the shallow water up on to dry land.

A fish I had set out to catch, and a fish I had caught, but he would take no part in my dinner that night, for between me and camp lay three and a half miles of rough ground, half of which would have to be covered in the dark.

When sending away my 11-lb camera I had retained the cotton cord I use for drawing it up after me when I sit in trees. One end of this cord was passed through the gills of the fish and out at his mouth, and securely tied in a loop. The other end was made fast to the branch of a tree. When the cord was paid out the fish lay snugly against a great slab of rock, in comparatively still water. Otter were the only danger, and to scare them off I made a flag of my handkerchief, and fixed the end of the improvised flagstaff in the bed of the river a little below the fish.

The sun was gilding the mountain tops next morning when I was back at the pool, and found the fish lying just where I had left it the previous evening. Having unfastened the cord from the branch, I wound it round my hand as I descended the slab of rock towards the fish. Alarmed at my approach, or feeling the vibration of the cord, the fish suddenly galvanized into life, and with a mighty splash dashed upstream. Caught at a disadvantage, I had no time to brace my feet on the sloping and slippery rock, but was jerked headlong into the pool.

I have a great distaste for going over my depth in these submontane rivers, for the thought of being encircled by a hungry python is very repugnant to me, and I am glad there were no witnesses to the manner in which I floundered out of that pool. I had just scrambled out on the far side, with the fish still attached to my right hand, when the men I had instructed to follow me arrived. Handing the fish over to them to take down to our camp on the bank of the river, I went on ahead to change and get my camera ready.

I had no means of weighing the fish and at a rough guess both the men and I put it at 50 lb.

The weight of the fish is immaterial, for weights are soon forgotten. Not so forgotten are the surroundings in which the sport is indulged-in. The steel blue of the fern-fringed pool where the water rests a little before cascading over rock and shingle to draw breath again in another pool more beautiful than the one just left – the flash of the gaily-coloured kingfisher as he breaks the surface of the water, shedding a shower of diamonds from his wings as he rises with a chirp of delight, a silver minnow held firmly in his vermilion bill – the belling of the sambur and the clear tuneful call of the chital apprising the jungle folk that the tiger, whose pug marks show wet on the sand where a few minutes before he crossed the river, is out in search of his dinner. These are things that will not be forgotten and will live in my memory, the lodestone to draw me back to that beautiful valley, as yet unspoiled by the hand of man.

from *Man-Eaters of Kumaon*
by Jim Corbett

AMERICA
&
CANADA

AT THE MOUTH OF THE KLAMATH

Upon arriving in Seattle from Vancouver Island we sent our Tuna Club light tackles home by express, reserving only the fly rods and casting rods we expected to use on steelhead trout in Oregon. And this circumstance seems wholly accountable for the most extraordinary fishing adventure I ever had, up to that time. It happened on our way home, after the beautiful Rogue River, with its incomparable steelhead, had captivated us and utterly defeated us, and when we had given up for this trip.

Leaving Grants Pass, Oregon, we visited the remarkable caves west of there, and then journeyed on over the Cascades to Crescent City, on the coast. I have no space here to tell of that beautiful ride and of the magnificent forests of redwoods still intact in northern California.

Some miles below Crescent City we came to a quaint little village called Requa. All we knew of it was that it was the place where we had to ferry across the Klamath River. The town perched upon a bluff, high over the wide river, and appeared to have one street. A long low white tavern, old and weather-beaten, faced the sea, and the few stores and houses were characteristic of a fishing village. Indeed, the place smelled fishy. I saw Indians lolling around on the board walks, and as we drove down under the bluff toward the ferryboat I espied numerous Indian canoes and long net boats, sharp fore and aft.

We had to wait for the ferryboat to come across. While watching the wide expanse of river, more like a bay, I saw fish breaking water, some of them good heavy ones. Next I heard two young men, who were behind us in a Ford, talking about fish. Whereupon I got out and questioned them. Fish! Why, Requa was the greatest place to fish on the coast! In justification of their claim they showed me three Chinook salmon, averaging thirty pounds, and several large steelhead, all caught that morning in less than an hour.

"What'd you catch them with?" I inquired.

"Hand lines and spoons," was the reply.

Then I went back to our car and said to the driver, who was about to start for the ferryboat:

"Back out of here somehow. We're going to stay."

R.C. and Lone Angler Wiborn eyed me with slow-dawning comprehension. They were tired. The trip had been long and hard. The drive over that dangerous road of a thousand sharp curves had not been conducive to comfort or happiness. And on the whole they had been very much disappointed in our fishing. The end of September was close at hand, and we were due to arrive in Flagstaff, Arizona, on the 29th for our hunt in the wilds of the Tonto. I appreciated their feelings and felt sorry, and rather annoyed with myself. But obviously the thing to do was to take a chance on Requa.

"Only one day, boys," I added, apologetically.

"What for?" queried R.C.

"Why, to fish, of course," I replied.

"Ahuh!" he exclaimed, with a note of grim acquiescence.

Lone Angler's face was perfectly expressionless, calm as a mask. He looked at R.C.

"Sure we're going to stop. I knew that all the time. I was just waiting until the Chief smelled fish."

"But we haven't any tackle," protested R.C.

I had forgotten that. Assuredly our trout tackles were not fitted for Chinook salmon.

"Maybe we can buy some tackle," I said. "Anyway, we're going to wet some lines."

Whereupon we went back to the inn, engaged rooms, got our baggage and tackle out of the car, and after lunch proceeded to investigate Requa in reference to things piscatorial.

Verily it turned out to be a fishing village, and the most picturesque and interesting one I ever visited. But all the tackle we could discover in the several stores were the large spoons and hand lines which were used there. We purchased some of the spoons, but the hand lines we passed by. Next we got one of the storekeepers to engage a launch and two skiffs, and men to operate them for us, and somewhere around three o'clock we were out on the water.

I drew a long flat-bottom net boat, which was a great deal easier to handle than one would suppose from looking at it; and the young man who rowed it was employed in the canning factory. He did not appear to be communicative, but he did say that the tide was going out and that the morning incoming tide was best.

The day was not propitious. With the sky overcast, dark, and gloomy, and little fine gusts of rain flying, the air cold, and the wind keen, it did not appear a favorable or opportune enterprise. I regretted subjecting R.C. and Lone Angler to more privation, discomfort, and work. Not that they were not cheerful! Two gamer comrades never pulled on wet boots in the dark of dawn! As for myself, I did not really care – the thing to do was to try – no-one ever could tell what might happen. So we made ready to troll around that bay.

Lone Angler had found a steel rod, which he equipped with a trout reel full of light line, and he waved that at me with these enigmatical words: "Now fish, you Indian! We got here first!"

R.C. and I had found two green Leonard bait rods that had been made for me some years before and had never been used. They were about nine feet long, slender and light, but remarkably stiff, and really unknown quantities. I had ordered them to try on bonefish, but had never used them. For bass they would have been ideal. I had a good-sized reel half full of no. 6 linen line, and to this I tied the end of two hundred yards of braided silk bass line. For a leader I used one purchased at Campbell River for tyee salmon, and selected a moderate-sized steelhead spoon with two hooks. Thus equipped, and with misgivings and almost a contempt at my own incomprehensible assurance, I began to fish. I did not look to see what R.C. put on his rod. I knew he was doomed to catastrophe, so it did not matter.

My boatman rowed me down the bay, not, however, very near the mouth of the river. But I could see that the bay constricted, with a high rocky bluff, almost a mountain, on one side, and a wide sand bar on the other. Evidently the mouth of the river was narrow. I heard the boom of surf and the scream of sea fowl.

There were several other boats out with fishermen dragging hand lines behind them. Here and there on the yellow, rather muddy surface, fish were breaking. I trolled up and down and around that bay until I was thoroughly cold and tired and discouraged, without a strike. R.C. and Wiborn had no better luck. We went back to the inn, where a warm fire and good supper were most welcome.

After supper I went over to talk with the storekeeper. He struck me as being part Indian, and I had confidence in him. I have Indian blood in me. I told him of our luck. He advised me to stay and try the incoming tide, early in the morning. He said the outgoing tide was no good for fishing. So after considerable argument with myself I decided to stay.

"Boys, go to bed early," I said. "Tomorrow we'll try again."

Next morning was clear. I saw the sun rise. What a difference it made! The air was crisp and clear, invigorating, and the day promised to be one of Indian summer. We got to the boats early, before anyone else was down. The man with the launch had not arrived. Lone Angler said he would wait for him, while R.C. and I took out one of the long skiffs. I found it very easy to row.

Requa and the mouth of the Klamath did not seem the same place as yesterday. All the way down the bay I marveled at the difference. Could it have been wholly one of spirit? The sun was bright on the dancing waves. Fish were breaking everywhere. Pelicans were soaring and swooping and smashing the water. Myriads of sea gulls were flying and screaming over the long sand bar. Low and clear came the sound of the surf.

I rowed straight for the mouth of the river to get into that narrow channel, where my adviser had earnestly solicited me to go. Before we got down to it I was struck with the singular beauty of the place. Huge cliffs, all broken and ragged and colored, loomed over the west shore of the channel, and on the eastern side the long bar ran down to a point where I could see the surf breaking white.

"Say, some place!" exclaimed R.C., as he turned to look ahead. His eyes lightened with enthusiasm. "Fish, too . . . Gee! look at that splash!"

When we got to the channel we found it to be several hundred yards long, and perhaps a hundred wide at the narrowest part. It was not straight, having a decided curve. A swift current of dark green sea water was running in, to be checked by the pale yellowish muddy water of the river. There was a distinct irregular line extending across the channel, the line of demarcation where the fresh water contended against the incoming tide of salt water. There was indeed a contest, and the sea was slowly conquering, driving the river back. In this boiling, seething maelstrom salmon and steelhead and cohoes were breaking water. On the point of sand a flock of seagulls were gathered, very active and noisy. They were flying, wading, standing around, some of them fighting, and all of them screaming. Black cormorants were diving for small fish, and everytime one came up with his prey in his bill several of the gulls would charge him and fight for his prize.

I took everything in with quick appreciative glances. How glad I was I had elected to try this morning! The charm of the place suddenly dawned upon me. Looking out toward the sea I saw the breakers curl green and sunlit, and fall with a heavy boom. Along the rocky point of the channel there was a line of white water, turbulent and changing, the restless chafing of the waves. And that river of dark ocean water, rushing in, swelling in the center, swirling along the rocks, and running over the sandy bar, assuredly looked as dangerous as it was beautiful.

"New sort of a place for us, hey?" inquired R.C., gazing around.

"Never saw the like. What do you make of it?"

"Great!" I exclaimed. "I'll bet we break some tackle here."

I rowed to and fro along the edge of the incoming tide several times without R.C. getting a strike. Then I said: "I'm going to get out into that tide. You let your spoon down to where the salt and fresh water meet."

R.C. looked dubiously at the swelling green current, as if he thought it would be hard to row against, and perhaps not safe. I had found that the big skiff moved easily, and I had no trouble getting out fifty yards or more right into the middle of the channel.

Almost immediately R.C. yelled: "Strike! – Missed!" Inside of a minute he had another, and hooked the fish. It began to leap. "Steelhead, by Jove!" he shouted. I rowed out of the current, back into the river water, and watched as pretty an exhibition of leaping fish as one would want to see. This steelhead cleared the water eight times and fought savagely. R.C. handled him rather severely. After he had landed the steelhead I rowed back into the channel and R.C. let his spoon down into that frothy melee of waters. "This won't be much fun for you," asserted my brother. "Fish!" I yelled. It was not easy to hold the boat in one place. Only by rowing hard could I keep even with a certain point. R.C. had two strikes, one of which was very heavy, but both fish missed the hook. Then he connected with one, a fish that kept low down and pulled hard. I rowed with all my might, holding the boat in the current while R.C. fought his fish. But I gave out and had to drift back into the dammed–up river water, where my brother soon landed a cohoe.

"Let's try anchoring out there," suggested R.C. "Maybe we won't stick. But we can't drift out to sea, that's certain."

This was a good idea. Promptly rowing back to the same position, and then twenty yards farther, I dropped the oars, and scrambling to the bow threw over the anchor. It caught and held in perhaps twenty feet of water. The boat swung down current, and straightening, rode there as easily as a cork. We were amazed and delighted. R.C. let out his spoon, down into that eddying, fluttering rip tide, while I took up my own tackle to get it ready. This was a moment of full content. No hurry to fish! I gazed around me, at every aspect of this fascinating place, as if to absorb it with all senses. I saw that the attractive features were all increasing. The sun was higher and brighter. The sky had grown deeply blue. Thousands of sea fowl were now congregated on the sand bar, and their piercing cries sounded incessantly. There the sea could not be forgotten for a moment. How the green billows rose higher and higher, to turn white and spread on the strand! The surf was beating harder, the tide coming in stronger. Foot by foot the yellow water receded before the onslaught of the green. How strange that was! These waters did not mix. Music and movement and color and life! Every time a rosy, shining steelhead leaped near the boat I had a thrill. I felt grateful to him for showing the joy of life, the need of a fish to play and have a fleeting moment out of his natural element. Yet I also wanted to catch him! This was not right and I knew it, but the boy in me survived still and was stronger than all the ethical acquisitions.

Still the biggest. Miss Georgina Ballantine's 64lb Tay salmon.

Major A.W. Huntington belonged to a select club of three members who had taken two 50-pounders from British waters (the other members were Professor Merton, a Wye specialist, and H.G. Thornton, see page 49).

Above: Harold de Pass celebrates the capture of a 50-pounder from the Awe, assisted by his wife, August 1937. *Below:* Mr Thornton's first 'portmanteau', 56lb, photographed at Malloch's, June 1923.

A big fish specialist of the 1930s. The late Anthony Crossley en route to the River Em, Sweden, and some of his catches. The single sea trout was the 1932 record, just under 28lb.

'Tiny' Morison with her 61lb record fish from the River Deveron,
21 October 1924, the largest taken on fly in British waters.

Recently found in Derby, this painting bears the inscription: "Portrait of a
Salmon caught at Llantrifsent near Uske AD 1782. Wt 68½lbs." How the
fish was caught, and by whom, remain a mystery.

BARONET'S BIG CAPTURE ON THE TAY

23:10:23 · 53 lb.

The record salmon taken from the Tay this season, measuring 49 inches in length and 27 inches in girth. It was hooked with a " Dusty Miller " (6-0) on the last day of the season in the " Pot Shot," Cargill water of the Tay, by that ardent and skilful fisher, Sir Stuart Coats, Bart., of Ballathie, and was landed after a fight of thirty-five minutes' duration. It is a very shapely male fish, and in exceptionally fine condition for the time of the year. The salmon is half an inch greater in girth than the 64 lbs. record salmon caught by Miss Ballantine, Caputh, on the Tay in October last year. This is the second fish, of over 50 lbs. that Sir Stuart Coats has caught, a feat seldom equalled by any fisher.

A HUGE TWEED SALMON

Said to be the third largest salmon caught in this country, the big fish seen in the picture is from the Tweed, and on sale in a Westminster shop. It weighs 65lb., is 53 inches long, and has a girth of 30 inches.

LOCH LEVEN TROUT. Dec. 16: 22.

Dec 16: 22 A 13½ lb. SEA TROUT FROM LOCH MAREE.

The above reproduction from a photograph shows a magnificent Sea Trout caught in Loch Maree on the 17th July last by Dr. John W. Mackenzie of Inverness. It was a most perfectly shaped male and fresh run. The weight of this race trophy was 13½lb., which constitutes it the record sea trout for Loch Maree. The measurements were as follows:—Length 32½ in.; Girth 18 in.; Depth 7½ in.; Wirth of tail 8 in. A cast of this grand trout has been made for Dr. Mackenzie by Messrs. W. A. Macleay & Son of Inverness, to whom we are indebted for the excellent photograph.

A page from Miss Ballantine's scrapbook. She maintained a special interest in big fish exploits, receiving many letters and photographs from fellow anglers after her record catch.

Mr Edward Cochrane of Paisley with the record Loch Lomond salmon, 44lb,
which he caught at the age of 83 in 1930, trolling on the Claddich shore.

Danish tobacconist D.C. Dinesen with his 58lb 'Anniversary' salmon from Jutland, Easter 1954 (see p.181).

Above: Martin Skorve (gillie) with the great 59lb Evanger salmon caught by Dr J.R. Holden in June 1949 (see p.7).

Left: The 'prawn trick' accounted for A.B. Ashby's Norwegian 58-pounder, August 1951. A.B. Ashby's son Michael explains: "The trick was to let the reel go the instant there was the smallest jerk on the line, and let the smitten prawn drift down in the current whereupon usually within three to five seconds there would be a convincing take."

June 18 1966. Arthur Oglesby with his first big salmon from Norway, 46lb.

Left: Terry Golding's Vosso 49-pounder (p.12).

Below: A 50-pounder taken on fly by the Duke of Roxburghe, River Alta, 1979.

Left: Twelve-year-old
Rupert Ponsonby with his
splendid 14lb sea trout from
South Uist caught in 1965.

Right: An early starter: Michael
Smith, aged eight years, with his
Tay salmon of 34lb, caught on a
"Lucky Louis" in March 1987.

Above: Odd Haraldsen heading upstream on the Alta, Norway (see p.151).

Right: Georg Stromme of Voss, Norway, had his portrait painted after taking two salmon, 64lb and 55lb, on one day from the Liland beat of the R. Vosso, June 1954.

Shark, 2176lb, caught at Hermanus, South Africa, by Mr W.R. Selkirk (see p.169). *Inset:* "It came as a Big Surprise" (p.187).

Right: Lilla Rowcliffe with her Spey salmon of 45lb 3oz, Delagyle Beat, September 1980 (p.56).

Below: Alison Faulkner with her 22lb Falkland sea trout (see p.173).

A 19lb brown trout from Loch Arkaig, 1972.

"Wow!" yelled R.C., jumping up with his green rod wagging. I heard his reel whiz. "Did you see that son-of-a-gun? . . . Goodbye to your green rod!"

The fish broke water on the surface, but he did not come clear out. I saw the pink color of him and part of his back.

"Big steelhead. Pull him up to the boat," I said.

"Aw!" That protest was all R.C. made. Perhaps he wanted to save his breath. For he certainly had all he could handle in that swift water. The steelhead did not jump or run; he just stayed down at the end of that mill race and defied R.C.

Fifteen minutes had passed when I inquired of my brother if he intended to land that fish so I could put my line overboard. No reply, but he risked my rod a little more! Meanwhile I saw the queer flat launch with Wiborn coming down the bay, and after it half a dozen skiffs. R.C. paid no attention to them. He was intent on landing his steelhead. I did not think he ever would do so. What a terrific strain he put on the slender green rod! It bent double and more. Gradually R.C. worked that stubborn fish close to the boat, and there we had our trouble, for when, by dint of effort, he got the steelhead nearly within reach of my gaff, the swift current swept it away. Naturally I grew excited and absorbed in our fight with him, and did not look up again until we finally captured him – not a steelhead, after all, but a ten-pound cohoe.

When we had him in the boat we looked up to see the launch close at hand, and a fleet of eight or ten skiffs anchoring or about to anchor right in front of us. For all we could see, there was only one rod in that formidable crowd, and that was a long flimsy buggy-whip sort of pole in the hands of a girl. Her boatman was a young fellow who could not row, that was certain. They looked like tourists, bride and groom, perhaps. I hoped they would hook a good-sized salmon, but I knew if they did they would never catch it. Several of the skiffs kept coming on, and actually got in front of us, ready to let anchors down where R.C.'s spoon was twirling. This was terrible.

R.C. and I were trained in a school where an angler respects the rights of others. Besides, to use Lone Angler's favourite expression, "We got here first!"

R.C. yelled at them, and finally they reluctantly rowed out of direct line with us and let their anchors down somewhat to our right. Next my driver and his man, who had brought us down from Seattle, came splashing along in another skiff, and they anchored even with our position, not twenty feet distant. Lone Angler, coming in the launch on the other side, laughed at us. "Ha! Ha! You'll have a fine time – if you hook a salmon."

R.C. looked at me and I looked at him with the same thought in our minds – that here was a perfectly wonderful morning spoiled almost at its very beginning. Only a matter of twenty yards of the channel lay open, and that was to our left under the cliffs. All the space to the right was covered by skiffs with anchors and heavy hand lines down. What chance now had we to catch a fish? There were Indians in these boats and white natives of Requa, all probably fishing for their livelihood. We could see that they regarded us with friendly amusement, as if they would soon have some fun at our expense. Soon see the delicate little rods smashed!

"Reckon we're up against it," said R.C. soberly. "Hard luck, though. What a grand place to fish, if those ginks weren't here!" "If we hooked a heavy fish now we'd not have one chance in a thousand, would we?" I queried, hopelessly.

"I should say not," replied my brother. Then suddenly he called out: "Look! Lone Angler has snagged on to something. Gee!"

Thus directed, I saw Wiborn frantically hanging on to his little black rod. The launch was below us to our left. The fish he had hooked – most manifestly a big one – was running fast across the channel straight for the anchored skiffs. Plain it was to us how our comrade was suffering. Usually a skillful and graceful angler, here he was bent out of position, hanging on to his rod with both hands, obviously thumbing the reel with all his might, in an effort to turn that fish. In vain! The rod nodded, bent down, straightened – then the line broke, and Lone Angler fell backward into the cockpit of the launch. R.C. and I had to laugh. We could not help it. Humor is mostly founded on mishaps to others! Lone Angler rose from his undignified position and seemed divided between anger and sheepishness. What a disgrace! When he saw us waving our arms he waved back at us. "He was a whale!"

R.C. and I were next attracted by the commotion in the skiff nearest to us. My driver was a Greek named Pappas, and fishing was new to him. His companion must have known still less. From the yelling and rocking of the skiff, and wild action, I gathered both of them had hooked fish at the same time. At any rate, they were frantically hauling on their hand lines. The lines became tangled, but the boys kept on pulling. They got in each other's way. Something broke or loosened. Pappas nearly fell overboard and his friend, stupidly holding his limp hand line, made no offer of assistance. Finally scrambling back to safety, Pappas entered into a hot argument with his companion, and they almost came to blows.

Next, one of the natives in a skiff hauled in a good-sized salmon, and others had strikes. Then suddenly the girl angler with the buggy-whip rod had a strike that nearly jerked her overboard. She screamed. The rod went down, and evidently under and around the boat. The fair angler did not seem to want to catch the fish, but to get rid of the rod. Her escort took it, holding an oar at the same time, and when he managed to stand up the fish was gone.

"What do you know about that?" queried R.C., ruefully. Manifestly it was no unusual occurrence to hook big fish at the mouth of the Klamath.

For answer I let my spoon drift down into the place where the salt tide was more and more damming back the fresh water. No sooner had it reached the spot when a heavy fish hit and began to run off with my line.

"Pull up anchor and grab the oars," I yelled. "We'll follow this bird."

R.C. lost no time, and before the fish had half my line off the reel we were following him. He swam straight through the narrow opening between the cliff and the anchored boats, out into the wide waters of the bay. There, by careful handling of the light tackle, I brought this fish to gaff in twenty minutes. It proved to be a Chinook salmon weighing twenty-two pounds, the first of that species I had ever caught, and certainly large enough to inspire and lure me back to try again.

As we rowed back past the skiffs some of the natives called to ask us to show our fish. R.C. lifted it up. They were outspoken and fine-spirited in their tribute to the little tackle. We anchored again in the same place. Conditions were perceptibly changed. The current ran swifter, fuller, with more of a bulge in the center. It lifted our skiff, and I knew that soon the anchor would drag. The sea was booming heavier behind us, and the swell of the waves now rolled into the channel. All the lower end of the sand bar was covered with water. Yet still the black cormorants and the white gulls contended for the little fish. Their screams now were almost drowned by the crash and wash and splash of threshing waters. Still farther back had the dark-green tide forced the yellow river. There was a mist in the air.

R.C. and I let out our spoons together. This time they drifted and sank, down to the margin of the tide. Something hit my spoon, but missed the hooks. I was about to tell R.C. when an irresistibly powerful fish ponderously attached himself to my spoon and made straight for the skiffs with their network of anchors and hand lines.

"Oh, look at him!" I wailed, as I tried to thumb my reel. It burned too severely.

"Good night! I knew it was coming. But stay with him till your hair falls out!" cried my brother, as he swiftly reeled in, and then jumped to heave the anchor and get to the oars.

When he had done so and was backing the skiff down the channel all the two hundred yards of silk line was gone off the reel, and the green linen line was going. My fish ran straight for the boats, and then apparently began to zigzag. Not the slightest hope had I of saving either fish or line. It was fun, excitement, even if no hope offered. R.C. had risen to the occasion. If my line had been round a hundred anchors he would not have quit. Lone Angler appeared beyond the skiffs and he was watching.

"Whatever you do you must be quick," was R.C.'s advice.

The whizzing of my reel began to lessen. I calculated that was because the line had become fouled on some of the anchor ropes. We cleared the first skiff. My line stretched between the anchor rope of the second skiff and the skiff itself. I had to pass my rod between skiff and rope. It went under water. I heard my reel handle splashing round. Both natives and Indians were helpful, both in advice and with their efforts. They all pulled in their hand lines, the nearest of which was wound round my line. What a marvel it seemed that my fish apparently stopped pulling while we untangled my line from the big lead sinker and spoon on that hand line! But so it actually was. The next skiff had out a long slack anchor rope. It appeared that my line had fouled this deep under the water. I put my tip down, tried to feel the line, then dipped my rod under the rope and lifted it out on the other side. Wrong! I had only made a loop around the rope. I had to laugh. How futile! Yet I did keep on – did not surrender. I dipped the rod back again, and then the second time. The line came free. It begun to run off my reel, faster and faster. There was only an inch of thickness left on the spool.

"I'm a son-of-a-gun if I don't believe we'll get clear," said R.C., giving in to excitement.

I had not yet awakened to any new sensation. Foregone conclusion had it been that I would lose this fish.

But I stood up and looked ahead. To my amaze my line was out of the water for a long distance ahead of my rod. Then I saw a man in the last skiff, standing up, holding my line high. It was slipping through his fingers.

"I got you free of my line. You're all clear now. He's on – and he's a whopper," called this fellow.

Impossible to believe my eyes and ears! I saw this fisherman, a big brawny man, bronzed by exposure. His face bore an expression of good will and pleasure and admiration that I will never forget. Somehow in a flash it electrified me with the idea that I might catch this fish.

"Look out, you'll fall overboard!" warningly shouted R.C. "Brace your knees on the seat. I'll catch up with that son-of-a-gun!"

R.C. began to row fast, and fortunate indeed was it that he had grasped the situation. For as he got into action, I glanced at my reel to see only a very few laps of the green line round the spindle. I turned cold. For an instant my right hand seemed paralyzed. Then I began to reel in readily. With sinking heart I watched it, sure, painfully and dreadfully sure, that my fish had gotten away. Why had I given credence to a futile hope? Why had I been so foolish as to surrender to a wild dream? He was gone. Then the line suddenly came so taut that the reel handle slipped out of my fingers and knocked on my knuckles.

"He's on yet. Row fast. If I can only get back to the silk line!" I called.

R.C. saved me there, and very soon I had all the green line on my reel. With the stronger silk line to rely upon now I had more and more irresistible hopes. I could not help them. To hook that tremendous fish, whatever it was, to get safely through that maze of skiffs, anchors, and hand lines, to feel the silk line slipping on my reel – it was unbelievable, too good to be true.

R.C. rowed perhaps three hundred yards beyond the last skiff before I could get enough line in to feel safe. Then we took it more easily, and gradually I got so much line back that I knew the fish was close. In fact it soon transpired that he was directly under us, swimming slowly. This was good, and I could not have asked for more. But when he turned and swam back toward the skiffs – that was another matter. It made me sick. It began to worry R.C.

More and more I thumbed the reel. The rod bent in a curve so that I had great difficulty in keeping the tip up. I did not dare look often at the rod, because when I did I would release the strain and the fish would take line. At times it would be nip and tuck. Then when I held him a little too hard he would make off toward the skiffs and the channel. In time he led us back to within fifty yards of the danger zone.

"Hold him here or lose him," said R.C., sharply. "No use to follow him farther . . . Be awfully careful, but hold him. That rod's a wonder or it would have broken long ago."

I stepped up on the stern seat and desperately strained every nerve to perform the most difficult task ever given me in an angling experience. To hold that fish, to check him, turn him and lead him without breaking rod or line, seemed an impossible achievement.

I elevated the rod and shut down on the reel. Slowly the arch of the rod descended, the line twanged like a banjo string, and just as something was about to break I released the pressure of my thumb and let the fish have a few feet of line. Then I repeated the action. Again!

"Row just as slowly as possible," I admonished R.C. "Not back, but across, quartering the current. Maybe that will turn him."

R.C. had no answer for me then. He rowed with great caution. And the fish gradually worked down toward the other skiffs at the same time that our boat was moving across the current. I could see all the other fishermen watching intently. We were close enough for them to see clearly our every move. From somewhere came Lone Angler's call of encouragement.

For me those moments were long, acute, and fraught with strained suspense. How many times I closed down on the reel I never counted, but they were many. My efforts to continue this method could not have lasted long. My arms ached and my right hand became almost numb. I grew breathless, hot, and wet with sweat, and when my eyes began to dim from the strain of nerve and muscle I knew the issue was short.

My fish had just about reached the zone of the anchored skiffs when almost imperceptibly he began to sheer to the right. Not a minute too soon! R.C. let out a pent-up whoop.

"We're leading him," he said. "Careful now. Only a little more and we'll be out of danger."

I had stood about all I could stand of that strain, so that even if the fish did come with us a little it was not easy for me. Gradually we worked him across the outlet of the river, behind the rocky bluff into wide placid waters. There I let him swim around until I rested my aching arms and cramped hands. Soon I felt equal to the task again and began to work on him. In the deep still water I soon began to tire him, and in half an hour more he came to the surface and wearily leaped out, a huge Chinook salmon. Eventually he gave up and we lifted him aboard.

Then I was indeed a proud and tired angler.

"Good Lord! Look at that fish – to catch on a bass tackle!" exclaimed R.C.

Broad and long and heavy, silvery and white, with faint spots and specks, and a delicate shimmering luster, with the great sweep of tail and the cruel wide beaked jaws, he was indeed a wonderful fish.

We rowed back to the point to exhibit him to the interested spectators, and then we went ashore on the sand bar to take pictures. It was all I could do to lift him high enough. Fifty-seven pounds! That was not an excessive weight to lift with one hand, but I was exhausted.

R.C. and Lone Angler refused to compete with me any more that day. I heard R.C. speak in an undertone to Lone Angler, and what he said sounded something like, "Hope he's got enough this trip!"

This I pretended not to hear, and I told my companions to take a last look at the most thrilling and fascinating place to fish I had ever seen. The world is wide and there must be innumerable wild beautiful places yet unexplored that await the hunter and fisherman. Of these I am always dreaming and creating mental pictures. Yet the waters a fisherman learns to love always call him back.

Requa, the fishing hamlet, quaint and old-fashioned, picturesque and isolated, stood out on the bluff above the Klamath, and faced the sea apprehensively. By the sea it lived. And its weather-beaten features seemed to question the vast heaving blue.

Down under the bluff the river was damming against the encroachment of the sea, and now the green water was slowly receding before the yellow. Ebb tide! The salmon and steelhead had ceased playing on the surface. But the glancing ripples were still there, the swooping pelicans and the screaming gulls, and the haunting sound of the surf.

From *Tales of Fresh-Water Fishing*
by Zane Grey, 1928.

THE SULKING SALMON

The first yearly canoe trip up the Grand Cascapedia from Middle Camp is always full of interest, for the topography of that part of the river changes from year to year.

As the thermometer often registers 30° below zero in the winter, much thick ice forms, which breaks up during the high water in the spring, and causes great havoc in this part of the river on its journey down stream. Pools come and pools go, for an ice jam, or a log jam, will sometimes change the course of the stream, and perhaps fill up an existing pool, or create a new one.

The banks of the river are torn away in places and you may not find the tree with the overhanging branches, where you parted company with the down-stream travelling big salmon of the previous year. It may have vanished, or else may lie a sad wreck at the head of the first rapids below.

Islands are sometimes formed by these jams, in fact there is now a large island, bearing upstanding trees, at the identical spot where a celebrated pool called Alman's was once located.

The river as a rule does not grow in width, but the channel changes, and the land makes where the old channel once ran. It is at first stone and rubble, but, with high water and during rain storms, soil is washed down from the banks of the river, and during the low water season vegetation begins to mend the wounds.

The great force of running water is in full evidence, but

sometimes it has been of benefit to the angler; for he may find a new pool where a shallow spot had been the year before. This is always interesting, and a keen joy when the first fish is taken there.

On my first trip up stream last summer, I heard that a new pool had been formed by an ice jam at the upper end of an island that is one mile above Middle Camp.

At the upper end of this island the river divides. On the eastern side the waters run shallow, too shallow in low water for a canoe to navigate; but on the western side of the island there is a long, fast-running rapid that feeds two good pools below. The first is Commodore, named after Commodore Bourne, and the second is Doctor, a tribute to Dr Weir Mitchell of fond memory. Above the island is Van Alen, once a good pool but now too shallow to be of service to the salmon.

It was close to the point of this island that the new pool had been formed. I fished it the first evening with good results, taking four fish that averaged 24½ pounds – 22, 21, 23, 32. Late in the evening I rose a big fish several times but he refused to take any fly that was offered him. As it was getting dark and I was cold, I ordered the killig up and we paddled home to a late dinner.

The moon was just rising over the eastern hills as we arrived at the Camp and I was greatly impressed by the beauty of the scene. The river makes a turn just there and the dark pines on the far side of the beautiful pool 424, as yet untouched by the silvery rays of the moon, formed a strong contrast to the smooth waters of the eastern side of the pool which was bathed in bright moonlight.

I slept the sleep of the just. My last thought was of the big salmon that had fooled me, and my first thought on awakening was one of fear that he might have left his resting place, and moved up stream during that beautiful night.

Rastus, my bow-man, asked me where I wanted to fish. I told him I wanted the big salmon that had spurned me the night before, so we started up stream.

Two strong men can pole a Gaspé canoe up stream about as fast as a good walker can walk along a river path, that is, if the rapids are not too frequent and too strong.

We passed Harvey's Rock, fought our way up Morancy rapids, and, as the water was high, went up the eastern and easy side of Alman's island to the new pool.

It was a beautiful clear morning with a gentle south-west wind blowing, an ideal fishing day. There was just enough wind to ruffle the waters and hide the movements of the angler, yet sufficient to cause an evaporation of the water, and to cool and aerate it, and supply the salmon with oxygen and good spirits.

My fur-lined short fishing coat was comfortable, for the air was crisp and it was air of a quality only to be found in the northern woods, health-giving air that you feel you can bite into.

The river was in full spring beauty. The pines and the spruces made a dark background for the tender young leaves of the maples and silver birch trees.

The Oenotheras were in bloom along the banks of the river, and many of the bushes were decked with white blossoms.

The birds seemed to appreciate the beauty of the day, for every now and then a kingfisher would fly past sounding a note that reminded one of the purr of a salmon reel. A mother sheldrake with a large brood of newly hatched ducklings struggled up stream, encouraging her young to follow her at a pace that was difficult for them to accomplish. When she had made up her mind that she could not avoid her approaching enemies, she hustled her brood into the bushes and then flew up stream alone landing on the river with much commotion in the endeavor to distract our attention from the place where she had hidden her young. As the canoe approached her, she soared high into the air, well out of gunshot, and returned down stream to her hidden ducklings.

There were both red and grey squirrels swimming across the stream as they often do. One day last season we saw numbers all swimming west and could not understand the reason, until the following day a forest fire many miles to the eastward of the river was reported. The squirrels must have scented the smoke long before we could.

I was fishing the Ledge pool that day with poor success, when a small and very exhausted red squirrel climbed up the stern of the canoe and sat himself down on the stern board facing us.

I was taking sea trout at the time, and when the stern-man would assist the "priest" in giving absolution to a trout, the squirrel would slip over the side holding on to the gunwale with one tiny paw and watch the proceedings with one eye.

99

When the dead trout had been deposited in the bottom of the canoe, he would return to his former position.

There he sat for an hour or more. Before we started for home, the stern of the canoe was backed up to the bank of the river and the squirrel scampered into the woods, but sad to say we, without thinking, landed him where he had come from instead of where he was bound for.

There are three short drops in the newly found pool. I took three salmon that weighed exactly 22 pounds each on the first two drops, without seeing any evidence that the large fish was still there.

When I had nearly fished out the last drop, there was suddenly a great commotion in the water and I found I was fast to a heavy fish. He slowly took a turn around the pool and then suddenly made for the rapids.

I shouted, "Rastus the killig, foul hooked, by Jove!" Just then the salmon jumped at the edge of the rapids, and I saw that he was a large fish and apparently fairly hooked. He started down the rapids at railroad speed and took most of my line before we could get properly started. My line felt very thin and my reel looked very empty, but, with a couple of strong strokes of the paddles, the canoe went sailing down the rapids after the fish. We were then evidently travelling faster than the salmon could swim, for my line became slack and I had to "coffee-grind" and longed for a multiplying reel.

We were half way down the rapids before I was on terms with the fish. Then I found that my line led up stream and thought it must be foul. I shouted to the bow-man and he directed the canoe into a luckily situated little backwater, three quarters of the way down the rapids.

I now understood that the salmon was sulking in a deep hole between two rapids and I was delighted – delighted because it was my first experience with a sulking salmon. Being a sea fisherman, it is my habit not to give a hooked fish one moment of rest, so I fancy salmon cannot often sulk with me, but this fish had taken advantage of the unavoidable slack line and probably thought on reaching this deep hole, that he had gone down-stream quite far enough; or, perhaps, he was suddenly reminded of his up-stream struggle in navigating these very same rapids and was not inclined to undertake it again.

The fish would not budge, and, as I said, I was delighted, for, although I had no experience with sulking salmon, I had well thought out my mode of procedure under such circumstances.

It was quite impossible for me to change the direction of pressure on the fish, for the canoe could not be moved without either fighting its way up stream or drifting quickly down the rapids, and there was no place where I could land.

My bow-man wished to stone the salmon, or to try to stir him up with a canoe pole; this I objected to. After the men had exhausted all their propositions I told them I would show them how to move the fish.

I had provided myself with several large snap-rings, such as are used to hang rubber curtains around shower baths. I snapped one of these on the rod just above the reel, turned the rod over, lowered the tip, and allowed the ring to slide down the rod and line to the salmon.

The effect was instantaneous. The big fish came to the surface at once and started to swim up-stream. I kept the line taut but put as little strain as possible on the tackle, for I knew no salmon could pull the drag of that line against such a strong current.

The fish fought his way gallantly up-stream for about one hundred feet, and then came floating slowly back tail first and drifted into the still backwater a thoroughly exhausted salmon. I nursed him to the canoe and he was promptly gaffed.

He proved to be a fine fresh run male fish that tipped the scales at fully 35 pounds. The eight salmon from the new pool weighed 199 pounds, a goodly average of about 25 pounds each.

Since that experience, I am never without a supply of curtain rings.

From *Fish Facts and Fancies*
by F. Gray Griswold, 1923.

THREE WEEKS LATER

Three weeks have passed, and many a salmon has been entered in the score-book at Red Camp. Mr Heckscher has killed his bear; Mrs Davis, a forty-four-pound salmon: and now the little party, standing at the landing, is about to start forth on its last day's sport together, for Napoleon, having decided to remain, is to join me on the morrow in the club fishing. As the sky is bright and the breeze fair, we are all up early for our morning's sport. It is my turn to fish in front of the camp. Pushing from the landing, the canoe is soon resting at the head of one of the best pools on the river for late fishing.

"Hello! there's one already," exclaims James. "Look – what a whirl! Be careful, Mr Davis; the water is clear. About thirty feet will reach him."

Casting toward the shore until the thirty feet are out, I send the no. 3 double Black Dose straight to the spot. A splash, and he is on.

"How splendidly he took the fly!" exclaims James.

"Bravo! bravo!" shouts William. "The first cast and – a salmon!"

Up and down stream, across, now back again, all kinds of antics does he kick in the bright, cool morning until we have him lying on the bank – a thirty-three-pounder. Paddling out again, the killick is dropped in about the same place; but although we see a large fish rise, I fail to lure him, as he probably prefers to continue his morning slumber. Drifting a short distance down-stream, a few casts are made to the right, when, suddenly, something enormous rises from the bottom, and, as it disappears beneath the surface, the delicate dark leader is carefully watched. Gradually it begins to sink. Now the hook is sent home, for I know the fly has been seized.

"Good Lord, what a salmon!" cry the men, as his broad tail strikes the water – a forty-five-pounder sure.

"Keep the canoe as it is, James, until you know what he intends to do. I cannot move him. Quick! up-stream. He's off! Whew! a run of forty yards without a stop. There he jumps! Faster, James!" I cry. "He is among the rocks! The leader will surely be cut."

"Give him the butt, sir, and turn him, if you can."

The rod bends and "He has gone!" I cry. "No, he is on; he is coming back!" Down the river he rushes, darting across the current and disappearing to sulk in thirty feet of water.

Dropping below the fish, we cross to the other side, and, paddling up-stream, hold the canoe in readiness beside the ledge.

> "To win thy smile I speed from shore to shore,
> While Hope's sweet voice is heard in ev'ry breeze."

"He can't stand that strain much longer, Mr Davis."

"Nor I, either, James. Look at the tip; it is three feet under water."

"Don't let up, sir; he will soon give in. Yes, there he comes now!"

Slowly the rod is raised, and, looking down into the depths of that deep pool, I see a bright form boring steadily downward.

"Now he's coming up, sir; pull a little harder."

Gradually the huge fish comes to the surface and, with a tremendous leap, tries for the current; but the struggle has been too severe: the spark of life has fled. So, gently drawing this beautiful creature toward me, I thrill with joy when the river-goddess finds a safe resting-place in my canoe.

"Have you ever seen so large a salmon, James?"

"None that was killed with a fly, sir; but my father tells of one which was speared many years ago weighing over sixty pounds."

"Well, let us go to the house now and see if this one has lived luxuriously; for should Dame Fortune be kind and bring the scale down to the fifty-pound notch my ambition in life will be fulfilled and my happiness complete. Lift gently, James – forty-eight, forty-nine, fifty pounds!" I cry. "Hurrah! the spring marks fifty, and the fair one's broad dark train still sweeps the ground."

Then, laying her upon a fern-covered bier, we tenderly bear her to the dining-room and gaze with admiration and regret on the splendor of her raiment and symmetry of form. Even Mixer [the dog] realizes that something unusual has happened as he stands in the awed presence. Presently Mrs Davis and Napoleon come in for breakfast, each with a fine big fish; but at the sight of this beautiful river-goddess both exclaim:

"Ned, did you kill that salmon?"

"Yes; and now, after trying to do it for thirteen years, I wish you were the guilty ones instead of me."

This fish was hooked just before seven o'clock and landed soon after. Its weight, at the Cascapedia station several hours later, was fifty and one half pounds.

I will not weary my readers with the story of my other large salmon, taken the following year. It weighed fifty-one and one half pounds fifteen hours after it had been killed. The salmon was hooked about eight-thirty o'clock at night, but owing to the lateness of the hour we were unable to gaff the fish until a few minutes after nine.

It was most unfortunate that the scales in camp were not heavy enough to have weighed these two large salmon, for they must have lost two pounds or more before they arrived at the station.

They were entered in the score-book as weighing fifty-one and fifty-two pounds.

From *Salmon-Fishing on the Grand Cascapedia*
by Edmund W. Davis, 1904.

IRELAND

THE NORE

One August some years ago now, I was again staying with my friend whose estate lies on the banks of the Barrow, in the County Carlow, on my way to the lakes of the County Clare.

Some may remember that it was here, at a spot near a large poplar tree, just below the attractive house, with its ivied front and climbing roses, that I had the misfortune to lose one of the biggest trout with which I have ever been in contact. Why, I often ask myself, do I lose these super-fish? Is it some failing on my part or just bad luck? For with salmon it has been exactly the same. Never, though several times attached to them, had I succeeded in killing a thirty-pounder. Once I was very near it. But in spite of wishful calculating as to loss of weight, 29½ lbs was the scales' irrevocable decision.

The broad Barrow still stretched like a gleaming silver sickle towards the distant blue peak of Mount Leinster, but now alas, owing to intensive dredging higher up it resembled pea-soup and there were but few trout left in this part of it. If, therefore any serious fishing was to be done, it would have to be further afield. Then it was I bethought me of the river Nore. This river, and a fine river it is, runs into the same estuary as the Barrow, and it is noted for its heavy salmon. In every normal season a few of exceptional size are caught in it.

Now, however, it was not of salmon but of trout that I was thinking. An article I had recently read, revealed that there were plenty of them, and of very fair average size. It might be worth trying.

Of course once the idea had entered my head, to the Nore I had to go. Enquiries showed that the nearest point on it was some seven or eight miles away, but having my car with me, this was nothing.

There had been fairly heavy rain, the week before, but now the weather was hot, and day fishing in August, except with upstream worm or minnow, being at a discount, I decided to pick a nice evening, start after tea, and fish late. When I say late, I mean till 11.30 or midnight.

With this project in view, I prepared everything beforehand, dry fly for the evening rise and a cast of three rails[1] for the dark.

Two days later, I set out fully armed, and provided with an excellent two-course supper of sandwiches (ham and jam) by my kind hostess.

The road was new to me, but after passing through a small town, I found myself on the banks of the Nore. Here I took a cross-road which appeared to follow the course of the river up stream. Sometimes I could see the water close at hand, at others it turned away and was lost to sight. Eventually, however, about 6.50, I came to what seemed a most attractive reach, running through grassy meadows. I stopped the car, got out and walked across a small field in which were a couple of cows, to get a nearer view. The river was a fair height owing to the rain a week earlier. It looked an ideal spot.

At my feet was a long flat of medium depth, shaded by a belt of high trees on the opposite bank; the very place for night fishing. Some distance up stream on my right, were some rocks, between which a heavy concentrated stream came swirling down, till it spread out into a a choppy length, and finally smoothed out into the flat by which I was standing. On my left was a bend which prevented my seeing the river, but I could hear the sound of rushing water.

I did not like to start without leave, and as I walked back, I wondered to whom the fishing might belong. On reaching the car I looked up the road, and there embowered in trees,

[1]Rail is the Irish term for sedge, as wet-sedges are tied there with landrail feathers.

was a large house. The owner, I felt, would almost certainly possess the fishing rights. So I drove on, found the gate and in three minutes was ringing the bell. A maid took my name and showed me into a large and pleasant drawing-room, and after a short delay, a distinguished-looking lady entered the room. With apologies for disturbing her I explained my object in calling. Now, in Ireland, all landed proprietors within a certain radius know one another and being acquainted with my host, she at once gave me leave to fish for trout whenever I liked. She even asked me to stay for supper. But fishing being my object I made the politest refusal I could, and departed with many thanks for her kindness.

Within a quarter of an hour, having donned my big waders and put up my rod, I was on the bank once more.

A few fish were already rising to a sparse show of large medium olives and before long I had a couple of half-pounders in the bag.

By this time the sun was getting low, and the real rise of the evening was starting. I therefore decided to put up the cast of "rails" which I had prepared. It was nowhere to be found. I hunted frantically through my cast case and even turned out my entire bag. It just was not there, though there were plenty of other things in it, which I did not need, or thought I did not. I must have left the cast at home, in the basin where I had put it to soak.

More and more trout were rising every minute. It was maddening. There was only one thing to be done – make up a new cast. Fortunately, one of my boxes contained a good supply of "rails" – but what about a cast? – Level 2X casts of which I had two already slightly frayed, would be too weak I thought. The only alternative was a good but not too new one, tapered to 1X, which had been in my cast case since the previous season. Rather heavy perhaps, but all right in the dark.

I soaked cast and droppers thoroughly, and in twelve minutes was ready to begin. The trout were now rising everywhere and some seemed to be of considerable size, but it was one of those mad rises, so aggravating to the fisherman, and all I caught were a couple, of about three-quarters of a pound apiece. However, there was still a good deal of light in the sky and I thought to myself, perhaps after dark they will begin to take in earnest.

Meantime, having noticed one trout which seemed larger

than the majority, rising persistently with a big splash in the tail of the heavy water I have described, I moved up to try for him. Several times I covered him, and many times he rose, but not to me. Then it happened. As my flies swung round for perhaps the tenth time, there was a great heave in the water, a gentle draw on the line, and I was fast. Fast in what? – my heart missed a beat – a salmon!

My first thought was, Thank God for the heavy cast, and also for having a good 70 yards of line on the reel. Then began a struggle in the dark which I shall never forget. At first the fish swam steadily up stream, nosing the bottom as if to take stock of this strange thing which had befallen him.

I have now caught quite a number of salmon when trout fishing, and it is my experience that the pressure of a trout rod is so light, that for a time a salmon does not realise that there is anything seriously wrong, and therefore does nothing violent.

So it was in this case, at any rate to begin with.

On reaching the head of the stream he lay perfectly still for a few moments, and nothing I could do would move him. In fact I thought he must have my line round a rock. Then he turned and started down the current at a fair pace, making the reel sing in short jerks.

I was using a 10 ft. 6 in. Palakona which is pretty powerful as trout rods go, but against his weight it seemed like a reed. Then the speed increased, and at the end of a short run, up he came to the surface and with a twist of his body dived down again. A really big fish. I caught the gleam of his side and it seemed vast. He must weigh 30 lbs at the least, and on a trout rod!

Meantime it was growing darker and darker and I did not know the water.

Now, without an effort, he was already 40 yards away in the shallows on the far edge of the flat. I could just make out his enormous tail, as he bored steadily down stream.

I held my rod high, fearing that at any moment the line might foul a rock. All went well however, and a sudden turn brought him head up into the deeper water in the centre.

He then started tailing down with the current, always a horrible process, and I followed anxiously. Round the bend we went, till in the semi-darkness I could see that we were rapidly approaching a line of stony rapids. On my side too a row of big trees on the bank effectually prevented further progress. This I thought must be the end.

Down, down he dropped until feeling the water shallowing he suddenly turned with a great splash, and with half his body exposed wriggled rapidly through the rapids and shot into the darkness of the pool below, making the reel scream. Fifty yards of sagging line were out when thank Heaven, he stopped! There was only one thing to do. The opposite bank was clear. I must take a chance and cross. And this I did, tripping and stumbling into deep invisible holes, and splashing myself to the eyes.

Then reeling in hard, I hurried down the firm grassy bank till I was opposite to where he lay, and with a sigh of relief felt that I was once more on terms with him.

After a few more moments, I lifted my bending rod, putting on all the strain I could to move him. It did – off he went in the fiercest run he had yet made to the very bottom of the pool. This was at least 50 yards long and as I guessed pretty deep. It was too dark to see now, but from the sound I was sure that below there must be a considerable fall. If he went over that, a break was a certainty, but at the very last minute he shied at it, swung round in a sweeping curve and raced frantically up stream again close under me with the line all loose. The next moment a dim silvery flash showed for a moment out in the darkness as the rush ended in a leap, and a slapping return to the water, which set the entire pool in violent agitation. Surprised that I could see anything I glanced up at the sky. There behind the trees a bright three-quarter moon was rising. That would be a great help. All the while, hoping against hope, I was frantically recovering line. But surely this time, he must be gone. No! He was merely taking it easy. I could feel the slow pulsing of his great tail. Then he accelerated and made a short spurt right up into the neck of the rapids but unable to face them, fell heavily back and drifted down stream. Keeping deep, he then began slowly to explore the big pool. Round and round he went at a steady pace with occasional jerks and shaking of his head, and against his sheer weight I was utterly powerless.

Ten minutes, twenty minutes, half an hour passed, till it seemed that we should be there till daylight. I looked at my luminous wrist-watch. It was 10.15, and I had hooked him at approximately 8.30! And then at long last he came to the top and rolled; that was a good sign. He was tiring. Moreover the moon was well up now and I could see better. I increased my pressure as much as I dared, and very, very slowly began to control his movements. Over and over again I got below him, and pulled his head round towards my bank, over and over again he countered me with that old trick of laying his head against the current and sliding out once more into the middle.

Gradually however, his circles became smaller and smaller and I began to think that if only the gut held, I really might land him.

And then for the first time – I had been too occupied to think about it before – it came to me as a shock, how on earth was I going to do it?

Everywhere the bank was distinctly high, and there was no suitable shallow on which to beach him. In any case, to tail a big fish in the darkness would be well nigh impossible. The answer came on the very heels of the question. Amongst the things which should not have been in my bag I had seen a small flat leather case, and within it was a small barbed gaff-hook with a screw end, given to me by a friend years before. That it fitted my landing net shaft I knew, for I had once tried it. It was not as sharp as it might have been, but at least it was a gaff. How to fix it and play the fish at the same time was another matter.

The first thing was to unscrew the net. This I found fairly easy to do with my right hand which was free. Once removed – for fear of losing it in the dark – I placed it over my hat, so that it hung down behind like an immense coarse veil. I confess I smiled as I thought of what my appearance would have been in daylight. Now came the much more difficult matter of the gaff head. My rod was in my left hand, and to avoid disturbing the fish I had to keep the tension as even as possible.

With a shake of my body, I swung the bag, with net-shaft attached, to my front, plunged in my hand and shook the gaff-hook from its case into the bag. To fix it would be much more difficult. First I tucked the shaft firmly under my left arm, which I held tight to my side, the screw part lying upward across my body. Very gently I inserted the gaff-hook and began to screw. Thank Heaven, it fitted and went home at the first attempt. A few turns and a final tightening with the aid of the left hand which held the rod, and all was secure. Then with what was now a gaff tucked firmly under my right arm, I was ready.

Meanwhile the great fish was slowly cruising round on the surface.

When I put on more pressure to bring him in, he resisted and moved heavily out a short distance, but the fight seemed to have gone out of him. As I turned his head towards me there was a kind of twang and for a second I thought the gut had parted. But in fact it must have caught in a tooth as the line changed position. Then he came sliding in alongside, I could see his white mouth gleaming dimly in the moonlight, as it opened and shut.

Leaning over as far as I dared, I gaffed him as deep as I could reach. Horror of horrors! the beastly thing had slipped on the tough skin, and away he went once more, making the reel shriek. But he was too tired to do much, and within five minutes I had him in position again. This time I decided to risk gaffing him in the jaw, a ticklish job with the line so near and in the dark. But as I judged, it was the only secure spot. Once more I saw his pale mouth open and shut in the light of the moon, and I struck. This time I had him. The commotion he made was terrific, and I was soused, but that did not matter.

Dropping the rod, I put both hands to the gaff, and hauled him up the bank, and well away from the river. Then I knocked him on the head. He was mine. I lit my torch and looked at my watch. It was 11.10! Then I turned it on the salmon. There he lay on the grass, a tremendous shape.

The biggest fish I had ever caught. Certainly over 30 lbs. By a sheer fluke my ambition had been more than fulfilled. The little gaff was firmly fixed in the tough muscles under the jaw, and owing to the barb, I had some difficulty in extracting it.

Only now did I realise that I was pouring with perspiration and deadly tired. Excitement alone had kept me going. My supper I had entirely forgotten. Passing a strong piece of string through his gills, I wearily dragged the fish and myself across the fields and through the river to the car. Then having packed up my traps, I ate a much-needed sandwich or two, lit a cigarette, turned on the headlights, let in the clutch, and made for home, tired but triumphant.

It was after midnight when I arrived and I let myself in as quietly as possible. After bestowing all the fish in the larder, I washed, and finished the sandwiches. Some hot coffee which had been thoughtfully left for me in a thermos, put new life into me, but I was dropping with sleep, and tumbling into bed as quickly as I could, knew nothing till the maid called me next morning.

At breakfast, in reply to my host's and hostess's enquiries as to sport, I made an evasive reply and said they should see for themselves. Their astonishment, as I had anticipated, was great. Several ounces over thirty pounds was the verdict of my steelyard. A truly magnificent fish, not at all red, and in remarkably good condition considering the month in which he was caught.

He must have come up the river very late. Thus was ambition accidentally satisfied.

It was unanimously agreed that under the circumstances not a word of my capture should be mentioned to anyone.

from *Fishing: Fact or Fantasy?*
by G.D. Luard, 1947

A Good Fishing Day
on the Shannon

I had by the time I am about speaking of become quite a proficient, but still dependent on the fly-tiers; I had been in Dublin, from whence I returned on a 15th of March, very well provided with gut, a good wheel, and good silk lines; and the day after went very early to Mr Dan Shaughnessy, and desired him to show me the sized hook then fished with, which he did.

I then insisted that he should make me four hooks two sizes less; when the following dialogue took place.

DAN   "Why, sir, these hooks will be too small, and they will float like corks."

O'G   "Don't mind that; I will pay you well, and you must do as I desire."

The hooks were made and turned.

O'G   "Now, Mr Dan, give me the plyers," which, on getting, I immediately applied to shaping the hooks my own way – perfectly straight from the bow down to the point, and the beard projecting very little. Dan declared they were the ugliest looking hooks he ever saw. They were tempered, pulled, and tried.

DAN   "Now, sir, what kind of flies will you have?"

O'G   "First, a black fly, with a deep yellow heckle."

DAN   "Such a fly was never tied."

O'G   "Don't mind that; it must be tied now, and on the least of the four hooks. Next, an orange coloured fly,

115

with a green silk tail, black heckle; next, a magpie, half black, half orange; next, a black fly, with an orange head – all with top knots; butterflies, dyed heckles, and jay cravats." I stuck to Dan until all were completed.

The next day was Patrick's day, and Dan was perfectly prepared for the celebration of the festival, it being quite useless to expect boat or boatmen, so that the fishing was put off to the 18th, and directions given to have a cot stationed before day on a large reach, called the tail of the lough.

We were out about eight in the morning: three excellent rods, the lines run out and well stretched, when Jack Kean, my chief boatman, requested that I would wheel up the lines, and then walked deliberately to the river. I asked what he was about, when he replied, that he was going to shave himself; and so he did, having lathered himself with a boiled potato – and, such a razor! By the time the operation was over his face was scarified like a crimped salmon. When he saw my flies, he regarded them with the utmost contempt, declaring that they were much too small and light, and offering one or two of his own, which I rejected.

We then commenced; the wind lying beautifully against the stream. We had taken many turns without success, and Kean was growling, and asking to put up larger flies.

I remained obstinate, though getting low sprited; when, casting my eyes down the stream, I saw, at about thirty yards from the boat, a large salmon rise. This circumstance could not be observed by Kean, his back being turned to the place the fish had risen in. Very soon after another, and another, in the same line. I said nothing, but was anxiously watching the time when, as I should judge, the flies might get among them, when Kean cried out, "You have him, sir!" We went ashore, and killed him rather easily. He was over thirty pounds weight. We had scarcely been out again, when we had two together; both large fish, which Kean and I killed. Out again, and not half way across, another, which we killed. In short, before three o'clock we had eight very large salmon killed, and had not lost one: the black fly with the yellow heckle having done more than its share.

We were now joined by Captain Cotter, of whom I have already spoken, and with whom I had made acquaintance. He insisted that we should go to a neighbouring house to lunch. This I objected to, though I was not at the time very knowing, for he did it for the purpose of taking me off the reach, and having it for himself the next day; but go we did, and staid more than an hour – I then insisted on returning.

When the captain saw my flies, he offered to back the black and orange, and the orange fly, half-a-crown each, against the yellow heckle fly. I took him up on each. Kean whispered to me, "Sir, there is no click to your new wheel, and it runs smooth and silent, so let out a little more line, that your fly may be a little below the other." I did as directed, and caught two more large fish. We now had ten; when it was proposed to fish the next stream, a very rapid one, called Poul a Herra. Here I was obliged to take the second oar, but keeping my yellow heckle fly still near me.

We had made several turns, and could scarcely keep the boat against the stream, when my rod had a tremendous pull. I instantly shipped my oar, and found, from the weight and strength of the fish that he must be very large. We, as usual, went to shore, at the Clare side of the Shannon, and, after about twenty minutes' hard and fatiguing play, he showed enormous; he was a new run fish, not long in the river. I brought him within reach of the gaff, when Kean made an attempt at him, and only scraped his back; away then he went across. We were again obliged to take to the cot, and follow him to the other side, and bring him back again, the banks at the Limerick side being high, and it being highly dangerous to attempt to gaff him into the cot in deep water. We at length killed him. He weighed forty-eight and a half pounds, and was the largest salmon I ever killed, though I have hooked much larger. Captain Cotter, in the month of May following, killed, with a fly on three-twist gut, on the stream of Donass, a salmon fifty-nine pounds weight: he was turning a little brown, but was a splendid fish. We then made another turn with much difficulty, and I killed another salmon with my fly, and the only small one we had, about eleven or twelve pounds weight.

This was the greatest day's fishing I ever witnessed. I have killed more salmon in a day; but to kill twelve, and no more hooked, without a single loss – of those, one of the weight I mention, three from thirty to thirty-five pounds weight, and all with one exception large fish – was, I believe, an occurrence in angling seldom paralleled: they were all spring fish, quite fresh run.

It was now late; no possible way of bringing home our fish but by water. We went down the river to the salmon weir, and having given some of the watchmen half-a-crown, got a basket taken up (there was no gap in the weir open on this day), and got safe to Ball's bridge. Cotter got three salmon, the cotman three more. Cotter lost eight half-crowns. I brought in six enormous fish to my relation's house, and so this unexampled day's sport ended.

from *The Practice of Angling particularly as regards Ireland*
by O'Gorman, 1845

GOOD NEIGHBOURS

Size is not the only source of the angler's curse, Envy

My water on the Slaney ran through a valley reputed to be peopled by fairies and my best pool was named the Fairy Seat. A high diagonal weir keyed on a boulder (which was probably the Seat) sent the stream slanting across to hit against the fore bank and run parallel with it over a nest of rocks which gave ideal lies. Standing on one identical spot I once hooked and landed in rapid succession four spring fish with not more than three or four casts intervening between landing one and hooking the next. My upstream neighbour, who was not devoid of jealousy, was watching through field glasses and her remarks were retailed gleefully to me next day by her companion. "Good, Kingie is in a fish." "My God, the judge has got another." "The bloody fellow has hooked a third." "This is too much, the bastard has a fourth."

from *A Man May Fish*
by T.C. Kingsmill Moore. (1960; 2nd Ed. 1979)

In The Money

If I ever could be satisfied with one place and one life I think that would be the south-west of Ireland. I love Africa with a peculiar love-hate. It has always been like that since the first time I went there and smelled the thick, musty sweetness which comes from the dust and the trees. I never smell that anymore. It is something you catch when you first step on African soil and it never returns. I have similar feelings about Ireland, but there is more love than hate.

I have spent many years in southern Ireland, particularly in Cork and Kerry. I first went there as a small boy when my father fished the Cork rivers for salmon and trout and I learned much of my fishing lore from a wizened pixie I shall here call Paddy.

Paddy was the most unorthodox man I have ever known. He could catch fish just as happily illegitimately as he would legally. I always believed that if Paddy had the choice of poaching salmon or catching them on licence he would poach them. He was a master poacher, something of a poet, much of a wit and an excellent countryman. He taught me all I know about salmon and trout, a little about pike and a little more about bass. Paddy understood and would tolerate sea angling but he was reluctant to accept the sport on an equal basis with game fishing and always said that a fisherman wasn't really a gentleman unless he fished salmon and trout.

Like any true ghillie, Paddy was a supreme snob. I have

known him refuse a good fee for a day as a ghillie because he considered the man wishing to engage him was not enough of a gentleman to be a game fisher. People who just wished to fish for sea fish and coarse fish were very low in Paddy's books. He always tried to persuade me from such practices but tolerated me because I was still a boy.

Paddy helped me to catch my first salmon. It was caught by pure chance but Paddy always protested that he had arranged it and he knew I would catch the fish. It was a very big salmon and I was very proud of it. It took three and a half hours to land and was caught on a sea-trout rod and a 4x gut cast mounted with a dry Greenwell's Glory.

We had been fishing the river since dawn and had taken two nice sea-trout and a dozen fair-sized browns. It was late in the summer and the sea-trout were running well. There were a few salmon in the river but because the water was so low, few had been caught and few anglers were seriously trying for them. Paddy and I had been working upstream from the brackish estuary waters and by mid-afternoon were well up the river where it ran through lovely riffles, pools and rapids between smooth boulders. It was one of those days the Irish so sweetly call "soft". It was mild with occasional fleeting sunshine and there was a pleasant dampness in the air from a light fall of early morning rain. The drifting clouds promised more for the evening.

We ate our lunch under a tree and Paddy sat for a long time afterwards smoking his pipe and drinking three big bottles of Guinness. He sat and watched me working my flies through the riffles and across the pools and gave me odd snips of advice.

A few fish dimpled the water but they were reluctant to take at this hour. Maybe they would take better when the evening came. Perhaps then I would catch some big sea-trout in the fast water with the wet flies. But under a water-dipping willow tree there was one persistent riser. He would suck down the flies as they passed over him and seemed to be taking everything which came his way.

I will try for this fish, I thought and moved carefully up to him. My first cast was well placed and dropped nicely above him. I mended the line so that the drift would take the fly straight over the fish and waited tensely. As the fly came over he came up. There was a suck, a swirl and the fly was gone. I struck quickly and the rod bowed over and the fish shot away as he felt the hook. He moved like a streak of lightning, shot right across the pool, through the riffle to the next pool and then into the shallow rapids. It was then that I saw him. Paddy saw him at the same time and let out a wild yell: "'Tis a salmon you have there," he cried. But there was no need to tell me that.

I ran as fast as I could in waders through the shallows and clambered over the rocks, following the fish up through the rapids to the calm water above. He was rapidly emptying the reel. It was a decent-sized fly-reel, a three- and-a-half incher with a big line capacity. Beneath the double-taper Corona fly line it held two hundred yards of 15 lb monofilament backing. But it was less than enough for such a big fish. Initially it was difficult to estimate its weight but we knew it was well into the twenties of pounds and maybe even bigger.

Trying to fight this fish was hard. Not only was there the constant worry of losing line but I knew there was every chance that the small fly hook would pull out or else the fine gut cast might break.

Anyone who has fought a big fish on a geared reel with adjustable clutch and who has complained how difficult and delicate it was, should try fighting a big salmon on a single-action fly reel which has no artificial aids. You play the fish by feel and allow him to run when you think he is pulling hard enough to break the line if you continue putting strain on him. It is a very basic skill which every fisherman should understand.

I once fought and killed an 83 lb tarpon off the West African coast on an old Hardy Silex and this is the only experience I have ever had which frightened me more than the salmon did.

When he was in the calm waters of the deep pool above the rapids the salmon began to shake his head and move up and down in steady surges. He did not attempt any long and fast runs. Paddy came hurrying along and I suggested he took the rod and fought the fish. I was terrified of losing it and I would rather have passed the rod over and seen Paddy catch it than lose it myself.

"No, my lad," Paddy said. "It's your fish and if you catch him you catch him and if you lose him 'tis all part of the game."

"But Paddy," I said, "it's worth good money – and think of all the porter it would buy."

"Indeed, that's true, my lad, so you'd better not lose it or else you'll be getting a thick ear from me and one from your dad."

Paddy sat down on a rock, lit his pipe again and let the warm smile ripple round his weather-beaten face. I set to battle the fish and kill it. I was determined to kill it.

The more it surged along the pool the more tired it became and after a while the surges became slower and shorter and I began to recover line. All the backing line was in and well over half of the fly line. I drew the fish so close to the bank that you could see him clearly in the water and Paddy murmured: "My God. He must be a good thirty pounds." As if he had heard and understood the awe in the old man's voice the salmon turned and shot away, ripping off line. He went back down the rapids, through the lower pool, down through the tail of it, through the next pool and into a fast riffle.

Here he hung in the current for a time and went through a few more surges. When I clambered down and came close to him off he shot again.

"He's away to the sea," said Paddy.

I slipped and slithered over wet boulders, my heart beating and my wrist aching from the pressure of the big fish. I held him when I could and let him go when he wanted to. I fought him every inch of the way but it was quite obvious that the salmon was taking me and I wasn't taking the salmon.

Finally, he came to a fast run which ended by going over a small waterfall. Here he made a spectacular leap and disappeared over the falls making the reel scream and giving me my first bad reel burn. The alloy drum spun against my hand so that there was a big red welt straight across the palm. I yelled with the pain but somehow kept on to the rod and even retained control of things. Then, with boyish disregard I splashed to the falls, filling my boots with water and leapt over. It was a drop of about six feet. I thudded into the pool where the salmon was resting. I landed with such a mighty splash that the fish shot off in terror, moved at an angle to the main run of the stream and ran aground on the shingle beach. There he flapped frantically trying to get himself waterborne again. I saw my chance, dropped my rod and dived on the salmon in a rugby tackle. I slammed my hands as hard as I could into his gills and dragged him further up the shingle. He thrashed and kicked. When I had pulled him away from the water I removed one hand from one gill, held him down with my knee and bashed his head in with a handy rock. I sat down beside him, soaked and bruised, my hands torn and bleeding from his gill rakers. I felt wonderful.

I was yelling at the top of my voice for Paddy and he came tramping over the shingle, his face beaming and red.

"Not so loud. I can hear you," he said.

"Did you see that fish, Paddy? Did you see the way I caught him?"

"Very unorthodox, that was my lad. Almighty God, you scared that poor fish so out of its wits it committed suicide. Not fair really, but I won't tell." He tipped me a wink, and slipped the gaff into the fish.

"There you are," he grinned. "Caught fair and square and gaffed it was." He swung the fish on the spring balance. It weighed thirty-three pounds and was fresh run and in fine condition.

"A thirty-three pounder on a trout rod is quite a thing for a lad."

"How much is it worth, Paddy? How much money will we get?"

"Well, me boy, that depends on your dad, but he should fetch six bob a pound at least and there's a fair few quid to be had. We might even give you a quid seeing as how it was you that was catching it."

"Do you really think so, Paddy?"

"Indeed I do."

Paddy slung a rope through the fish's gills and shouldered it. It always amazed me how Paddy could produce some necessary tool or gadget he needed whether it was a monkey wrench or a piece of string. It was there in the Pandora's Boxes which were his patched pockets. Paddy is no sea fisherman but once while sea fishing I lost all my leads and I was ready to finish when Paddy dug his hand into his trouser pocket and out came a five-ounce torpedo lead. It wasn't of the type I used and where he got it I shall never know. Paddy was *the* Irish character.

*In another fishing adventure with Paddy, the young
Pearson finds money changing hands once more.*

Paddy and I shared many things, but perhaps my favourite was
the day of the strand racing at Ballyclane when we caught the
big tope on the racing course.

We had gone to the strand to fish for bass and we had caught
fish through the flood and back down the ebb. In those days I
rarely used worm bait, but caught my fish with herring strip
and this was the bait I had on the hook at Ballyclane.

As the tide neared low water Paddy, my father and I were
standing there fishing when a large collection of men, dogs
and horses appeared and began to spread out over the beach.
A group walked towards us but before they arrived a fish took
the bait and ran fast making the old centre-pin reel scream. A
long way out it broke water, swirled and then jumped.

"My God," my father said. "It's a tope."

The little group reached us now and the leader, a big man
with a red face, tipped his hat to my father, scowled at Paddy,
who gave him a knowing but deadly wink, and said (to my
father) "Sor, excuse me but you are fishing on our racing course
and we are soon to be starting the racing." He then saw that I
was well fast into a fish and added: "But, sor, the lad must get
the fish in first, sor."

I began to fight the fish hard but he was taking some doing
and the struggle had attracted attention. Much of the interest
had now strayed from the strand racing to my fish. Even the
mounted jockies were among the gathering. The bookies were
taking bets on whether or not I would land it.

One man said: "But what about the racing, for soon the tide
will be flooding?"

And the red-faced man, who had taken off his jacket and was
stood at my right shoulder making punching motions as though
he were sparring up for a prize-fight while saying "Get it, lad!
Get it!" turned to the dissenter and told him that the racing was
of little importance next to this fish and if he dissented again he
would get his nose punched. A short while later I noticed that
the red-faced man had disappeared.

The fish was big and strong, but I had a lot of line on the
reel and he was well hooked and I could afford to take my time

with him. I fought him carefully and soon had him close to the beach. He was making short runs up and down the shore just behind the last breaker of the three-breaker surf, with his back fin and tail fairly visible. He was a tope of about sixty pounds.

With the fish close to landing, the excitement was intense and there were men rushing around in all directions, some on foot, some on horseback and all with a covey of snapping and barking mongrels at their heels. As the tope came into the surf wash they all dashed for it, including a jockey on horseback waving a long gaff and slashing madly at the fish. Behind him came the dogs and the dogs got the best of his horse which shied and threw him into the surf. The fish was finally seized by the local curate who dashed up to it in a splash of black ankle-length cassock, seized it by the tail and heaved it on to the dry sand. Some men yelled and some men groaned and money began to swiftly change hands. The tide had flooded quite a way and there would be no strand racing that day. But it was of no consequence. It had been a broth of a day and everyone was happy. It was my first tope.

It was only when the excitement had died a little that we realised the ubiquitous Paddy was absent. Drunk perhaps. Collecting his winnings maybe. I was sure he had backed me to win. Down the beach two men were fighting.

from *Fisherman*
by Anthony Pearson

ALMOST
IN
WALES

The Record Spring Salmon

The story should really begin about six weeks ago, for it was then that my mother suggested that I should go to Biarritz with her. I said I would rather stay here and hunt with the Radnor and West Hereford Hounds and catch some salmon. That was the start, for had I gone to Biarritz I should not have caught my big fish! Then came the day of the catch. Just as we started walking towards the river at Winforton, Mr Powell said to me, "Now, Miss Davey, you know what you have got to do today! Mr Merton has just got a forty-five pounder, Mrs Hope has got one about the same size, and so you have to catch one at least forty-seven pounds!" Just as I began to fish my father said to me, "Don't forget. If you hook a 'Monster' treat it with just the same disrespect as you would a twenty-pounder. If you get anxious and try to favour it you will probably lose it. That's how the big ones get off!" It was curious how I had the big ones so impressed on me that day!

The "Cowpond" begins, I believe, near my father's fishing hut, and continues downwards for about 200 yards of deep water with a strong current through it – good fly water with a rough stony bottom – until it bends into what is known locally as the "Middle Hole". The "Middle Hole" always holds fish, but only once in eighteen years has a salmon been taken there. It is a deep, broad, swirly place, and the fish run up from it into the "Cowpond", probably to discuss the weather, take the air and sometimes, I believe, to lure the angler! This one did so! I fished over him in the morning, for my father generally turns me on to the best places. The salmon was probably thinking of other things just then – perhaps of his coming honeymoon or of the vile wind which was blowing, for he would not come and join in the sport!

I fished all day, as did my father, but nothing would respond. At about 5.30 p.m., having lost all hope and fully expecting to have to go home and record another blank day, I was making a few casts while waiting for my father to join me, and I hooked a fish on a small minnow I had put on for a change. I adopted the usual tactics, but the fish just swam about and did more or less what he liked! I believe it is even possible that he growled at me, but a cold north-east wind drowned the noise and so I did not hear it! He had several nice bits of exercise, but he never jumped or let me get a glimpse at him, and I had to do practically what he suggested, for I was unable to make any real impression on him.

After about twenty minutes of this my father came along, and I called to him to take a turn. He put on as much strain as possible, and gave me the rod back again in about ten minutes, saying it was my "funeral" and so I ought to do the bulk of the work! So I went on again for about ten minutes and then we changed once more and my father did his best to make the fish really annoyed. We did not want him to go down the river any further, and he did not want to go up! We had been taken as far down the river as was safe.

Then we found that we could annoy the salmon best by walking him up the river with very hard pulling, and then running down with him. So we continued doing this as far as we were allowed to do it by the brute. Of course I was constantly varying the angle of the strain, so as to throw him off his balance, but he countered this by varying his position to meet what I was doing. And so it went on, and it grew darker as the twilight faded. I had to fight the daylight as well as the fish! Luckily the fish and the river were west of us and so we could see the line for quite a long time in the twilight.

Then, at last, about seven o'clock, he got quite cross, running down and across the river wallowing along the surface so that we could see him for the first time. Up to now we had only been guessing, but in the fading twilight we could see that it was really a monster reflected on the surface of the water. After this it soon got quite dark, and Jellis, father's chauffeur, had a brain-wave! He has been with us for about twenty years, we call him John, and he has gaffed lots of salmon. He started a large fire on the river bank, and got some paraffin and paper from the hut ready for the crucial moment when the gaff should be required. It was a "desperate fine battle", but the fish now had to do what we wanted him to do more often than when the fight started. We knew that if the hold was good and the tackle did not give out from the long continued strain, "beauty would defeat the beast"! An onlooker, who had never caught a fish before, gave us quite an amusing turn. He thought it was about time to pour some of our precious paraffin on the fire, thinking we wanted more light. There was no one to stop him, and he did it. I can smell that funny odour of singed cloth even now!

Then my father swore! He was taking a spell at the rod, and I went to feed the fire. The tin of paraffin had been left near with the cork out, and I accidentally kicked it over! I saved enough for the final effort, however, and father quietened down! We were joined by a fishing neighbour, Mr Barret, and Mr Merton's gillie, Charley Donald, who had come to see what the trouble was about, having noticed the fire and the figures moving about. They brought four inches of candle with them – bless'em!

The fish, by now, was making shorter journeys, and was "jagging" badly – a most disquieting action to the angler, for it feels as though every jag must break something! The only safe thing to do, I think, is to keep the top of one's rod well up, and rather easy, allowing the top joint to do what it was intended to do.

The end came with almost dramatic suddenness. The fish took a few long lunges, rolled a bit, ran, and was pulled to the right towards the bank. Jellis crept quickly to the right, but the fish saw him cross the firelight for he jinked, ran back and round to my left. He was steered in, and, in a mix-up of splash and spray, the faithful John Jellis with the gaff and Charley Donald with his hands as much round the tail of the fish as he could get them managed to haul him out of the water. The fish was landed at 7.35, and was hooked at 5.40! One hour and fifty-five minutes of concentrated excitement and real hard work! We never gave him a moment's peace, and played him hard the whole time

131

with the sort of strain that will kill a twenty-pound fish in seven or eight minutes.

Luckily for us Mr Powell, of Winforton, who kindly allows us to leave the car with him, formed himself into a "search party" and came to look for our corpses with a hurricane lamp – a thing anyone in our family is warned not to bother about under three days! However, we were very glad to see him and his lamp, for we were able to find our way back to the car. The fish was taken to the office of the Wye Board of Conservators the next day and was weighed and measured – weight fifty-nine and a half pounds, length fifty-two and a half inches, girth twenty-nine inches. The fish was then displayed in Hereford, an outline for a carving made, and the flesh was then sold, the proceeds to be given to the Herefordshire General Hospital.

I have had dozens of nice letters of congratulation from friends and complete strangers. Amongst the strangers, some have sent poetry and one proposes that I should marry him! However, this is another "catch" and I am not rising! So many people have written inquiring as to all the tackle, etc., that I may as well take this opportunity of satisfying their curiosity. Reading from left to right, or rather, beginning at the end where the worm fits on! – the minnow was a two inch aluminium of Hattons', Hereford, hook and mount also Hattons'. The line was an old and ridiculously thin undressed silk, supplied by Hattons' to my uncle, Lieut. J. S. Davey, who was killed at Ypres in 1914. This line killed a thirty-four-pounder in 1914, so you can tell that it was a good bit of stuff. The rod was a split cane made by someone many years ago who didn't know his job! Perhaps that is why my father gave it to me! But Mr Hatton has it periodically to make the joints good, and it looks quite all right and ready for another! The reel was a "Rolo", which I like immensely, and was a Christmas present from my father.

Now with regard to "the fool at the other end"! I started to fish when I was five years of age. That was with a bread pill for a roach in competition with my father. He used to beat me then. Now, as the Americans say, I have him cold! My father takes tens in boots, smokes Franklyn's Shag and has a catapult in his pocket except when he goes to London, which is not often!

I only once hooked a bigger fish and that was when we were trolling for pollack in Basentarbot Bay, on the west coast of

Scotland. It stopped the boat! The skipper shouted "Hard a-starboard" but father went hard a-port, as it was more natural to him! That fish said "Good-bye" and I must say "Good-bye" too, but not before thanking all my friends and correspondents for their very kind congratulations. I am indeed lucky!

Doreen Davey *Fishing Gazette*, 31 March 1923.

A Fighting Usk Salmon

On Friday, the 25th ult., a friend and myself went down to the Usk Association water between Llangattock and the Chain Bridge, he to fish and I to gaff, he being a member (a most desirable one too) who very rarely troubles it, having some private water above, which he fishes on alternate days with the owner. We both went without waders, knowing that the water was high, and that some of the pools could be fished readily enough from the bank. We arrived about eleven, and began to fish a long flat of some 300 yards or so – good, as Matthew Williams, the head keeper, says, in high water. However, in spite of the fascinations of a large Silver Doctor, with water looking perfect, though high, nothing happened, if we except a trout of a pound or so, promptly returned to the water. At the end of this flat there is a good pool, in which a gentleman was fishing, and who (his attendant told us) had just lost a fish of about 10 lb. Wishing him mentally better luck, we walked down to the next corner – a quiet pool, seven or eight feet deep, the tail end of a series of rapids, and a very likely place for a large fish at this season of the year. Immediately behind us the marly clay bank rose rather steeply; and under this, screened from the eastward, and with the sun upon it, it was pleasant enough. Plenty of willow flies were about, and the trout were rising pretty briskly.

My friend began to fish quietly and deeply, letting his fly sink well, and he suddenly felt the friendly tug under water, without seeing any symptom of a rise. He said, "I've got him." In Ireland, if you say "I've got him." they say to you, "Wait a bit, your honour." Here we say, "I'm in him." There is a considerable difference between the two; and so it proved here. We had not "got him" by a long way. My friend added that it felt like a small fish, some 8 lb or so; but, as he spoke, there was a great rush, and, about thirty yards away, out sprang a fish which we estimated at 20 lb or 25 lb. We now felt that business was beginning. I looked at my gaff, and, finding it rather shaky, having been made of bad stuff to begin with, asked a bystanding keeper to request the gentleman above to kindly lend us his, which he readily did. While the keeper was away the fish again made some frantic rushes, jumping out of the water five or six times. After this he settled down for five or ten minutes. During these calmer moments I administered to my friend a little stimulant, for by this time he had been holding on steadily and firmly for a good hour. I am able to state this, because when the fish was first hooked I looked at my watch, and it was 12.10 exactly. Time passed, and at 2.20, after making three or four more rushes, and when we thought he must be pretty nearly done, the fish set off full split for 300 yards down stream to the next pool, my friend following with sixty or seventy yards out. I expected to see him fall every moment on the greasy and steep bank, and I knew he had no nails; however, as luck had it, everything went well, and we came up smiling to the middle of the next pool. In the centre there was a big snag – a tree in fact – and our anxiety increased; to foul this would be fatal. By this time we had quite an audience – the gentleman who had lent us his gaff, his man, and two keepers. The only thing to do we all felt was to keep the salmon clear of this snag, and to get him on our side of it if possible. We managed this, the fish making, however, once right across the stream, a rush of at least sixty yards, and jumping out three times. The water below the pool was a very rapid shallow, 400 yards long – to me a very dangerous-looking place. At this crisis a gentleman who had been fishing below, and who had unfortunately broken his rod, came up, and advised taking the fish into the rapid that he might wade in, and, as the fish came down, gaff him. I thought the advice a mistake, being of opinion that it is much better to keep your fish in quiet water if possible; but, as he knew the water better than I did, I said nothing.

To guide him down the rapid being decided upon, and my friend having no waders, he asked the gentleman who had lent us his gaff to take the fish down to a certain point. This he did most successfully, putting on just sufficient strain, and guiding him capitally. I felt for him, knowing how trying it is to take another man's rod, and that man a stranger, for if the fish gets off, there are painful regrets on both sides. So far all right. In the meantime our other friend had got into the stream lower down, and was standing there "silent but ready", as keen as mustard. When the fish approached him, and was about five or six yards away, it saw him and rushed across the river far out of reach. Down below us was a very nasty-looking stone, over which the water boiled; and opposite the stone, the river being narrower here, was a large dead tree. Seeing this obstacle, we were all very down in the mouth, feeling sure that the line would foul this stone, and all would be lost. I felt that if this happened I must gaff somebody as a relief to my own feelings. Down came the fish, and in spite of all we could do, there was a foul round the stone! My friend quickly handed his rod to our former friend in need, and he, going in, most skilfully disentangled the line, and we heard – ah! what music – that the salmon was still on! Promptly our helpmeet with the gaff rushed fifty yards down stream, calling out to my friend, who had now re-taken his rod – the fish coming down stream all the time – to pull him, if possible, into a comparatively still bit of water and shallow. It was our only chance, as below the water was too deep for wading, and there were big willows, over which it was impossible to pass the rod. The fish was carefully brought to this spot, where our comrade stood with his gaff as still as a heron, and he gaffed him splendidly at the first attempt! I looked at my watch; it was 4.20!

We weighed the salmon at once. It was 30 lb, a cock fish, and red of course. I cut the Silver Doctor out of him myself, neither the fly nor the piece of single gut a bit the worse. The fish was hooked at the junction of the upper and lower jaws very slightly outside. I have fished for forty years or more, and have caught salmon in Norway, England, Ireland, Scotland, etc., and have never seen any fish behave like this. He sulked very little, but was perpetually fighting, and sprung out of the water fifteen times (I counted them); and he was on four hours and ten minutes.

C.W. Walker
from *The Field* November 1889

BIG FISH

The Wye is famed for its big fish, and many anglers who visit the river take a beat for the sole purpose of catching one. Now many of us have got into the habit of referring to a big fish as a "portmanteau" because the slow and irresistible movements of a very large fish when hooked feel to an angler as if a portmanteau or a dead donkey has annexed the bait; but before we proceed further it will be as well to define exactly what a "portmanteau" is. In many rivers a fish of 20 lb would be a big fish, but that is only an average weight for the Wye in spring. In summer the average weight of fish goes down. Mr Pashley writes to me as follows in regard to summer fish: "Below Ross I have known a rod kill over one hundred fish after May 1 in a season and not have a 20-pounder in the lot".

There are many large fish killed in the Wye between 30 and 35 lb, but they cannot be reckoned as really big fish, as "portmanteaux" in fact. They are merely "ladies' hand-bags" and can be dealt with easily. The "portmanteau" – that is the really big fish which imparts that feeling of an irresistible force – must weigh, in my opinion, over 35 lb at the very least, and nothing less than that weight can be called a really big Wye salmon. Numerous, by comparison with other rivers, as these big Wye salmon are, a man may fish the Wye for many weary years on end without catching one, and there are several instances of keen anglers who have fished the Wye for long periods without catching a fish even as heavy as 30 lb in weight, while many have tried for a quarter of a century and yet failed to catch a 40-lb salmon. Mr Pashley writes me about his first 40-pounder, which has now been succeeded by fourteen others!!

"My first 40-pounder was killed on Guy's Hospital water with a £2 season ticket! Like many others of like weight it met its fate by aid of a glorious fluke.

"I had hired a small pleasure boat from Davies (who, alas, was drowned at night a few years ago when going clotting for eels) and arranged to meet W.B.P. at the Dock at Ross. I fished the Weir End blank with a fly and then dropped downstream to Hom Pill, which is a deep, almost streamless hole. It was a blazing hot day for the 12th of May and my friend being a fly purist inquired what I thought of doing there. With hesitation the word 'minnow' was whispered. 'D——you and your minnow, I'm going to sleep,' he ejaculated, was curled up and had 'gone' before you could say knife! I discovered the spinning line was rotten and after removing the whole 100 yards dressed line was restricted to 40 yards of hemp backing at the bottom of the reel. At the tail of the pool the line tightened, which produced the usual 'I've got him'. A diminutive pleasure boat with a portly Chairman of a Board of Guardians suddenly awakened from slumber is no place for the rest of the crew, and it was just touch and go if she didn't capsize. We managed to survive the awakening and Davies was told to pull up the anchor and row after the fish as the line was too short to reach across the river. The fish swam majestically round and then made for the right bank, upon which I landed. Davies waded into the river and the fish sailed right up to him in the muddy water and the gaff was home almost before he realized he was in trouble. Directly Davies could remove his feet from the clinging mud of the river bottom and regained terra firma the sport began, the gaffing had taken place in a drinking place for cattle and he was up the track and over the brow like a streak, before I reached the top of the bank 30 yards were off the reel, and yelling to him to stop, was running to prevent the removal of the last ten yards and save a certain break. It was sheer waste of breath; he ran across the field like a hare towards the Ross and Monmouth road, then swinging to the left, never slackened pace till he laid his prize against the trunk of an ancient oak (still standing) 120 yards from the river! In due course my friend arrived with the boat's stretcher with which he laid open the 40-pounder's head; fit retribution – for disturbing his slumber or for taking a minnow!"

In my own case it took thirteen years of fishing to catch a salmon of over 35 lb and twice as long to catch one of over 40 lb; and many other fishermen have not been so lucky even as myself. The chances, taken for the river as a whole, against any particular fish hooked being a "portmanteau" appear to be the enormous odds of 120 to 1; and, great as these odds are, each fish hooked provides the excitement that it may be a "portmanteau" at last. In order to arrive at this estimate of the odds, I counted up some of the returns of the Wye Board of rod-killed salmon during the last twenty-five years, and found that, out of roughly 48,000 fish, about 400 were of the "portmanteau" variety and four only weighed over 50 lb. So that even while the chances against a "portmanteau" may be great, the chances against an "American travelling trunk", a 50-pounder, only four of which have been killed by Wye anglers, are the stupendous odds of 12,000 to 1, and few of us will ever live to kill a salmon as large as that. Since I began to fish for salmon, I have only seen five fish of above 40 lb in weight killed, while I have assisted in the obsequies of some thirty-odd salmon which weighed over 30 lb, and I admit that I have been very lucky indeed to do so. Fish of the "portmanteau" variety appear to move slowly up the river, and more of them are killed in the lower and middle reaches than in the upper. Therefore the chances against catching a very large fish vary according to the distance up the river. A large fish is more likely to be caught, say, in the Quarry Pool at Aramstone than in Hell Hole at Glanwye, but even those who fish low down the river may not be lucky with big fish. For instance, Mr Morland, of Foy, the well-known Wye fisherman, has sent me particulars of 1,531 salmon which he has killed in the last thirty years. He began to fish in 1896 during the netting times and, curious to relate, the very first salmon he hooked was a real "portmanteau". This fish took Mr Morland's minnow in the Carrots, and broke the trace. A fortnight later the netsman very politely handed him back his tackle with the tantalizing information that the fish out of whose mouth they had obtained it weighed 43 lb. Mr Morland had to fish the Wye for another seventeen years before he caught a fish of over 40 lb, and after that again he had to fish for fifteen years more before he caught a second. Mr Pashley, our star fisherman, however, has killed no less than fourteen fish of over 40 lb.

Well worthy of a place among the big fish of the Wye are two 30-pounders killed by the late Mr Graham Clarke at Glanrhos. These two fish, though not noteworthy for their size alone, are certainly worthy of record on account of the tackle by which they were killed. Mr Graham Clarke was using a 4-oz rod and casting a natural minnow with an Illingworth reel. The line was the thinnest cotton (breaking strain 2½ lb), and I marvel that Mr Graham Clarke managed to defeat these large fish with such light tackle. I do not know of anyone who has killed a salmon while trout fishing, but I have twice seen large spring fish take a March Brown on a small rod and cast; but in these cases the fight did not last long and the inevitable end came very quickly, as soon as the fish had run out all the line. My father, however, once caught a small fish of 12 lb while fishing for chub.

As regards the huge fish of over 50 lb, the first of which I have any record is the legendary monster which the Hon. Geoffrey Hill, and Christmas the keeper, played all through a summer night in the Agin Pool at the Nyth; but this fish was never even seen by the angler, and therefore cannot be included in the list of real big fish. Nor can that other great "fish" which a medico of Ross played all night long only to find in the morning that he had been anchored to a piece of fencing wire, the uneasy writhings of which had deceived him into believing they were the struggles of a salmon. Five fish only of over 50 lb have been killed in the Wye on the rod, and the full list is as follows; The first of these huge salmon weighed 51 lb and was killed by Mr J. Wyndham Smith in 1914. He killed this salmon in the famous Quarry Pool at Aramstone; and on the same morning he killed another fish of 44 lb. Two fish weighing 95 lb and this, I believe, a record for a single day's fishing in the Wye, as regards size.

In March, 1920, Colonel Tilney killed the second in Higgins Wood at Whitney, which weighed 52 lb, and thereby set up a record for size which lasted for three years, until on

March 13, 1923, Miss Doreen Davey broke the record again in the Cowpond, with a fish of 59 lb, and this record is still unbroken.

The Tale of a Wye Fisherman
by H.A. Gilbert, 1929

TALE OF AN UNSUNG SALMON

A startling black-and-white photograph is the only record left of a 51½ lb salmon caught in the River Wye in 1962. What a pity! If ever a fish deserves to be preserved by the taxidermist, surely it's a salmon in the 50 lb category.

The fish of dreams was caught by Cambridgeshire farmer Donald Parrish on the Lower Bigsweir beat of the Wye at Llandogo, near Monmouth, and a taxidermist did quote £75 as the fee for mounting the specimen in a glass case.

Unfortunately, in those days, Donald felt he couldn't afford the cost himself, but as the fish had been caught on all-Hardy tackle he drove it up to London and offered it to a representative of the famous tackle-makers.

Surprisingly, it may seem to some of us, Hardy's man declined – even though a massive crowd quickly gathered around the open car-boot and the police had to be called in to clear the obstructed pavement.

Goodness knows what interest the salmon would have generated had it been mounted and displayed in Hardy's window! Sadly, the salmon was eventually consigned to the smokers at Smithfield, leaving a snapshot as the only evidence of its existence.

The photograph was taken on the lawn of Brown's Hotel and tea-rooms in Llandogo and for almost 30 years has hung on the restaurant wall. Generations of salmon fishermen visiting the Bigsweir and Coed-ithel beats of the river have gazed in

fascination at the monster fish and wondered at the details of
its capture.

Mostly they've remained unaware that Donald Parrish has
often been sitting among them, still a member of one of the
local syndicates but too modest to announce that he's the man
in the photograph who once caught a 50-lb salmon and joined
a very exclusive band of fishermen.

Today Donald is 80 years old, but he still remembers clearly
the details of his record catch. It was Saturday, May 26, 1962,
and he was fishing from a stone jetty in the Station pool, just
below Bigsweir bridge that crosses the Wye midway between
Chepstow and Monmouth. He was spinning with a 2½-inch
red-and-gold Devon minnow, using 23 lb line and an 18½ lb
trace.

"When the fish took, it ran right across the river twice and I
worked it back," he says. "I was fortunate that it didn't choose
to go up or down the river. It wasn't a terrific battle. Indeed, it
was surprisingly easy.

"We saw its tail just once and the gillie shouted: 'You must
catch it, sir – it's a 40 lb fish!'"

The fish was played-out after only 15 minutes and gillie F.E.
Swann was able to gaff it. News of the catch quickly spread,
but after posing for celebratory photographs and recounting
his story to a score of eager listeners, Donald was faced with
the decision about what to do with his salmon.

"Frankly," he says today, "I was amazed at Hardy's attitude,
but they weren't the least bit interested. I'd thought the salmon
would have made a good advertisement for them. It had been
caught using all-Hardy tackle and, when my wife opened the
back of the car in London, and the fish was on view, a crowd
quickly gathered. It certainly created great interest, but the
Hardy's man just wasn't impressed."

At least before the fish was sent to be smoked, a detailed
scale-reading was made. This revealed that the salmon's sea-life
had been five years, and that it had probably weighed about 57
lb when it had come into the river, some six weeks before being
hooked.

Just for the record, even if it had been caught immediately
it came into the river, it still wouldn't have been the biggest
salmon taken from the Wye. That honour belongs to the 59½
lb salmon caught by Miss Doreen Davey at Lower Winforton in

1923. But Donald's fish was the biggest since 1939, when a 54 lb salmon was caught by Sir Thomas Merton, again at Lower Winforton, and it is believed to be the fifth largest ever caught in the river. It was certainly a fish of which any river would be proud, and it is curious that a photograph of Donald Parrish's salmon has found its way into the bar of a pub on the Usk, where locals lay claim to the fish having been caught in their river. Fortunately, in this case, the angler is still alive to put the record straight.

"I often get asked if I regret not having had the fish mounted," says Donald. "I suppose I do, but at that time it seemed like a lot of money. If I catch another 50 lb salmon I'll probably have it done this time."

If he does, he'll find the costs have risen almost tenfold in the past three decades.

A taxidermist, asked to quote a price for mounting a 51½ lb salmon, said he would charge between £590 and £734, depending upon whether you wanted a flat or bow-fronted glass case. The cost of having a cast made of a fish that size was put at £592.

Incidentally, using moulds for salmon of a similar size (caught in Canada and Norway) and with the detail from the photograph, it would be possible, even today, to make a very accurate replica of Donald Parrish's 51½ lb Wye salmon.

Is anyone from Hardy's listening?

Tony Gubba in *Trout & Salmon*

BIG FISH
SPECIALISTS

BELIEVE IT OR NOT

The late Mr Roderick Anderson, of Anderson Brothers, who had a fishing tackle shop in Princes Street, Edinburgh, and who happened also to act as the Hon. Sec. of the Curling Club to which I then belonged, a man from Dunkeld, and who often spoke to me of salmon matters of interest, told me one day that an old soldier who made baskets and fishing creels had caught a monster of a fish. He said that it had been caught illegally, and that the man came into the shop from time to time for orders. I asked him to telephone me the next time the man came, and to let him know that I would like to hear about this fish, also that the information would not be used against him but would be regarded by me as a matter of natural history.

It was three weeks or a month later when I heard that the man was waiting in Anderson's shop, so I went there at once. I found a tall man with a quiet, respectful manner, an evident old soldier, but not one of the wild sort by any means. The first thing to do was to establish friendly relations and confidence, after which the story came out somewhat after this fashion:

"There were three of us fishing the mouth of the Devon with a net, in the month of December, when we caught this fish." The Devon, I may explain, flows into the tidal estuary of the River Forth some miles below Stirling, and the date of the incident was 1901. "It took the three of us to lift it out of the water and it was the ugliest great brute I ever saw. It was quite black on the back and had an immense hook on its jaw and a

149

large head. We had nothing to weigh it with, but, of course, we knew that it was a quite exceptional fish, so we took it up to a neighbouring farm and got it weighed on the farmer's scales. We weighed it with great care and the nearest we could make it was 103 lb. and 2 oz."

When I asked what had been done with the fish, I learned to my great regret that it had been cut up and distributed, and that no outline or tangible record had been kept.

From *Salmon Fishing*
by W.L. Calderwood

BIG FISH CATCHER

(Odd Haraldsen)

Arthur Oglesby
Harrogate
N. Yorks
England

Oslo, June 1992

Dear Arthur,
In reply to your letter regarding the number of big fish being caught over the years, I can just have a theory about that.

It is certain that the number of these monsters show a similar picture, as the number of fish over all caught in Norwegian rivers. There is no doubt in my mind that this is due to the fisheries of the high seas with driftnets and long lines. You can just have a look at rivers in Norway over the last five years. This shows that the number of all fish has gone down considerably.

I simply do believe that the big fish are taken at the high seas, and not permitted to return to the rivers. Apart from

151

that, I am no expert, just having fished for salmon over 35 years now, and having obtained a few ideas about the salmon picture.

We have a good example in the river which I used to have for twenty years, from 1965–1984, when some foreigners came in with bids on the fishing of the Vosso, which simply was ridiculous.

It is hard for me to say whether their way of fishing or their lack of nursing the river, is the result of the very small numbers of salmon they have caught. It is, however, a certainty that the number of salmon taken in the Vosso river in 1991 was just a fraction of the average number of fish which was taken during my twenty years in the river.

I do, however, agree with you 100 per cent about your point of view upon the fisheries of the high seas. Stopping the anglers from using rod and line in the river do not, as you quite correctly say, improve the situation. It is after all small amounts of fish being taken by rod and line in salmon rivers.

One other of my theories about big fish not coming up anymore, and also the reason for the number of fish coming up, is of course due to the lack of police activities for prohibiting the netting in the estuaries and also further out at sea. Although netting has been considerably reduced, there is still poaching going on and unless the Norwegian government find money enough to employ people to control this poaching, I am afraid we shall have the same results in the years to come.

Now over to your question about the big fish I have taken. I have, as you will see, made a list, just to show the years and the weight of the fish. Should I take into consideration all the salmon I have taken, it would be a very long list. I therefore had to start somewhere, and I have started on 15 kg, 33 lb. You will see over the various years, how many I personally have taken. There are of course quite a lot of other people who have taken big fish in the Vosso, but not of the same amount as I have had.

I feel it is fruitless to describe the various fish, but there are of course a few of them which I remember vividly. The absolutely biggest was on 27 kg.

You will note from the list I have given you, that I have

taken fish of all weights, apart from 24 kg and 26 kg. Those are the only weights I have missed, as from 5 kg and up, including 27 kg. It stands to reason, however, that most of these big fish are taken either on spoon or prawn, mainly due to the depth of the river I have fished in, which may be up to 10–12 yards in some pools.

Talking of the biggest fish I have ever had on a fly, I have to refer to the one taken in Alta in 1981, the weight was 20.5 kg. On top of that, this was also a coloured fish, so its weight must have been considerably more, as it was taken in the beginning of August.

I do believe, however, that if you want to describe some of the big fish taken, you can always use your imagination and write anything you want about what happens when you have a big fish on. The fish going out, coming in, going out, going deep, jumping and everything. You can just use any description you want, and it will be no lies because that is what really happens.

Personally I must admit that I am a little bit tired of reading about all the various ways of playing a salmon when on. It is all the same, the line going out as I said etc. etc. and you are eventually sitting down exhausted on the shore, looking at this monster, glittering in the sun.

Odd Haraldsen

Fish over 15 kg (33 lb) caught by Odd Haraldsen

VOSSO	Date	Kg
	26.05.1965	23.5
	07.07.1965	27.0
	29.07.1965	15.0
	24.05.1966	22.5
	15.06.1966	18.0
	16.06.1966	15.0
	22.06.1967	15.0
	23.06.1967	19.0

VOSSO cont.	Date	Kg
	24.06.1967	16.0
	25.06.1967	15.0
	25.06.1968	17.0
	20.06.1969	19.2
	19.05.1970	18.0
	20.05.1970	17.0
	21.06.1971	15.0
	1972	0
	13.06.1973	21.9
	22.05.1974	19.0
	1975	0
	19.05.1976	15.25
	18.05.1977	19.75
	17.06.1977	18.5
	1978	0
	16.06.1979	15.5
	1980	0
	01.06.1981	17.0
	29.08.1981	25.0
	01.06.1982	19.25
		18.5
		22.5
	02.06.1982	20.0
	04.06.1982	21.0

VOSSO cont.	Date	Kg
	1983	0
	01.06.1984	18.5
	17.06.1984	16.5

OTHER RIVERS	Date	Kg
Jolstra	1964	19.0
Alta	1981	20.5
		15.5
Alta	1982	16.0
Aaroy	1965	18.0

Big Fish Reel

A Brake on the Winch:

What a splendid fighter is the mighty Mahseer. Though you have "foiled his wild rage" in the suddenness of his first mad burst, reducing rod friction by the use of a pliable rod that "stoops to conquer"; though you have been careful also to have as little winch friction as is safe; though you have in both these directions minimized uncontrollable friction as much as you can and dare, so as to have the better command of the friction which you can control and utilize, by raising or lowering the point of the rod so as to increase or moderate what I have called the rod friction; though you have done all this, still who has not wished that he had more power of friction at his command. Who has not felt that it is with all too light a heart that the mighty Mahseer laughs at your bending rod, that when the time has passed when you fear his suddenness, when the pace has slackened and you feel it is safe to begin to put on pressure, who has not felt that it is all too little that you have it in your power to apply, and that bend your rod as much as you dare, the fish is still going going gaily just according to his own sweet will. It is the burden of every description of Mahseer fishing that you read in the sporting papers, that the angler had no control whatever. In how many cases does he tell you that he put his hand on the line in the hope of checking the pace, but instantly had to withdraw it as the line burnt him like fire. Verily, it is exactly like fire, and he who has done it once will not do it again. With the line running at a pace that cuts a groove in the very brass ring at the rod top, won't it cut a burnt groove in your fingers if you touch it? Rather. *Experto crede*. Even a salmon will run out at a pace that makes a salmon fisher chary of putting his hand on the line without the intervention of a thick glove. How much more a Mahseer. But you cannot wear thick gloves in tropical climes. I have gone so far as to try thin white kid gloves. But they are not a bit of use. The flying line cut them through like a knife in a trice, and was burning my hand just as if I had nothing on. In no time the gloves were cut right through in half a dozen places, and no impression whatever was being made on that Mahseer. It was only I that was impressed. It vexed me so to think that he had the game all in his own hands, and I could find no way of being even with him, till at last I have devised a brake which gives you complete control over the friction, so that you can regulate it to a nicety and with the greatest promptitude. I had it made for me some sixteen years ago, before leaving India, and have tested it again and again on Mahseer, and found that in actual practice it works to perfection. It is no new idea with me copied from others. As long ago as my first edition of 1873, I had suggested what I then called a Mahseer drag, but which in my next edition I subsequently discarded as imperfect. But my present idea I am quite satisfied with after thorough trial, and can confidently recommend it to my brothers of the angle. Since coming home I have seen in tackle shops two other devices for compassing the same object, showing that tackle makers had accepted it as an end to be gained if possible, and if it is so with salmon much more it is with a Mahseer.

One of these tackle makers was himself a practical salmon

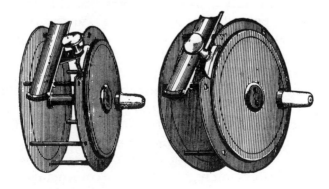

fisher, and assured me that he found by actual experiment, that he could kill a salmon much quicker with his device than without it, and I do not doubt him for a moment. Indeed, I can see that it must be so, for he has gone half way to getting hold of the same idea as myself, but stopped short at what has been my difficulty, that of applying a practical brake. As in my own winch he brings the revolving plate to the outside edge of the winch on one side, but there he gives it a smooth surface so that he can apply his finger to it to check its speed as it revolves. He says it succeeds with a salmon. Maybe it does. But I would like to see him trying the same game on a Mahseer. He'd very soon cry "off", with his finger burnt by the much more rapidly revolving plate, or if he relieved his finger by taking it off now and again, as a man does when trying to stick to a hot plate at a shooting lunch, and as I did when trying to stick to my trial of the white kid glove, the very taking off and on must mean want of continuity of pressure with occasional jerks, after one of which he would probably find that the Mahseer had cried "off", for any abrupt stoppage to a fish going at that tremendous pace must necessarily imply more or less of a jerk, and probably prove fatal. But with my brake it is not so. There is a comfortable hollow button handy to the finger or thumb-tip through which you can apply to the revolving plate just the modicum of pressure you desire, and can apply it continuously without the slightest inconvenience, and there is a spring which makes the brake spring free the instant you release it, or relax the pressure, so that you can regulate the pressure to a nicety from an ounce pull upwards to a dead lock, and that with promptitude, according to the varying tactics of the fish throughout the conflict, and by the pressure of a single finger.

The other device I saw was a screw on the outside non-revolving plate, by giving a turn to which you could bring pressure to bear on the side of the inner revolving plate, and so set the friction to any degree you liked. But so *set* it became a permanent quantity till you unscrewed it again, a thing you could not attempt to do while in the act of playing a fish. Any such *set* friction would be utterly fatal to Mahseer fishing. It is the very thing we have been trying so long to get rid of, *uncontrollable* friction, for though, in the case of this device, it may be capable of being regulated before commencing to fish, it is under no sort of control at the second of a heavy fish striking you, and would probably insure your being broken at the first blow, the critical instant when you want your pliable rod and your easily running winch to help you till the pace slackens, and till you dare to apply thoroughly *controllable* pressure.

If I thought of my brake sixteen years ago and thoroughly tested it on Mahseer, why, you will ask me, why didn't I tell brother fishermen of it through the medium of sporting papers. Why, because there was one thing wanting.

I had no manufacturer in India competent to perfect my winch, and when I came to England I forgot all about it till I was asked to revise this book.

I may mention here that my manufacturer thought to improve on my pattern by fixing the brake to the side of the reel, and keeping it free by a spiral spring, but it was a dead failure, just so much force being needed to overcome the spiral spring that you could not tell how much you were using against that, and how much against the fish, and it consequently spoilt the *nicety* of regulation of pressure on the fish. He thought my exposed spring likely to be injured, but when in use on the rod it is in a very well protected position.

If you use a brake and bring to bear on the fish more pressure than you dare ask of your rod by raising the point, it follows that you must lower the point of your rod more and more in exact proportion as you increase the pressure beyond what the rod could bear if not lowered, and so you may go on lowering your point and increasing your brake pressure, without any danger to the rod, till you get rod and line both in one and the same straight line from your hand to the fish. Then you are playing the fish by hand. This is a most extreme position, but on one occasion I was compelled to adopt it and only killed my fish by being able to adopt it.

H.S. Thomas
The Rod in India (3rd Ed. 1897)

BIG FISH RIVER

In its natural state the Awe was a short river, barely 4 miles long, linking the 22-mile-long Loch Awe with Loch Etive, a sea-loch, the mouth of the river being close to Taynuilt. It was thus very much a counterpart of the Ness and the Lochy, short though sizeable rivers, each of them draining a large loch, fed by headwaters. In the case of Loch Awe the main headwater was the river Orchy, which had a 16-mile course from Loch Tulla on the edge of the Moor of Rannoch lying to the north-east. But there were many other smaller burns which entered Loch Awe throughout its length.

The river Awe had an exceptionally steep downward course, dropping 116 feet in barely four miles, and that without any full-scale falls to contribute towards this abrupt descent. It was a comparatively narrow river, in fact, once it had left its outlet from Loch Awe at the Pass of Brander, its width rarely exceeded 25 yards except in one or two of its larger pools such as the Shallows and Fanans. But its current was fierce, and its bed extremely rocky. It was said to resemble one of the smaller types of Norwegian river, so rough was its downward plunge, and indeed this was not an unrealistic comparison. Together with that of the Orchy and the other feeders entering Loch Awe, the Awe's total catchment area amounted to 271 square miles – slightly smaller than that of the Findhorn, and about comparable with that of the North or South Esk, or the Beauly. But it was an infinitely faster and more powerful stream than any of these.

Stories about fishing in the Awe during the old days would

provide drama for several volumes. In the early 1900's and up to the 1939 War salmon averaged anything in weight between 16 and 20 1b. Forty-pounders were killed almost every season, and I have compiled the following list of as many Awe 50-pounders as I can trace, though no doubt it is not complete.

Weight	Caught by	Date	Where Caught	Remarks
57 lb	Major A.W. Huntington	July 8 1921	Cassan Dhu	Length 57 inches Girth 27½ inches Caught on a Mar Lodge 3/0
56 lb	Mr H.G. Thornton	June 12 1923	Pol Verie	Caught on a 5/0 Fly
55 lb	Mrs Huntington	Sept. 19 1927	Errochd Pool	Landed in Dalvarde
54 lb	Mr J.B. Lawes	1877		
54 lb	The Schoolmaster at Taynuilt	1880(?)	Cassan Dhu	Landed at Crubeg
53 lb	A. McColl (ghillie)	1913		
53 lb	Col. James Thorpe		Inverawe Cruive	
51 lb	Dr C. Child	Sept. 1907	Near Taynuilt	Killed on a "Blue Doctor"
51 lb	Mr A. Lees Milne	Oct. 1913		In the same month Mr Lees Milne killed other fish weighing 47, 44 and 42 lb
51 lb	Major A.W. Huntington	May 22, 1930	The Stepping Stones	Killed on a Green Highlander 2/0
51 lb	Mr H.G. Thornton	1934	The Seal	
51 lb	Mr H. de Pass	1936	Little Verie	

Is this not an amazing record? Maybe the Tay or the Wye could produce a longer one of 50-pounders killed, but it must never be overlooked that the Awe in length is just short of four miles! All these enormous fish, as well as 40- and 30-pounders infinitely more numerous, were killed on this astoundingly short extent of water, in contrast to the Tay's or Wye's near 100 miles.

Many of these big Awe fish were caught on fly; a big Green Highlander was a popular choice – though some on bait (sometimes prawn).

It is worthy of note that Major A.W. Huntington, also Mr H.G. Thornton, caught two 50-pounders here during their fishing career, a feat seldom equalled elsewhere in Britain.

And as to the capture of the 54-pounder by the Schoolmaster of Taynuilt, which he hooked in Cassan Dhu and landed in Crubeg, Grimble in his *Salmon Rivers of Scotland* (1899) writes as follows:

> I was out that day and met him at the Clay Pool on my way upstream; the fish was still going very strongly. I unluckily did not turn back to see the end of the fight, which eventually finished at Crubeg, the lowest pool on the water, and out of which it is impossible to follow a fish making for the sea.
>
> This was a right good performance, of which anyone might fairly be proud; only a tall active man could have carried it through, as in following from the Otter Pool into the Stepping Stones the water was up to the schoolmaster's chin, and at this part of the fight a man five inches shorter would probably have been beaten.

This was indeed a "right good performance" seeing that the schoolmaster, and one should take off one's hat to him, followed his fish for the best part of a mile down a broken and turbulent river, but so for that matter would have been the capture of any of the monster fish listed above. Anyone seeing for the first time the Awe's swift and rockstrewn course would wonder how even a 20-pounder could be successfully handled, let alone leviathans in the 40- and 50-lb class. The only hope was apparently to use very strong tackle, and to know beforehand of any particularly dangerous rocks or snags, making every effort from the start to keep a hooked fish clear of them. Even so in the case of fish of 30 lb or over it must have been odds on that a disaster would happen in one form or another, and the fish go free. There is no doubt that the majority of such fish when hooked were lost rather than caught. The hooking and playing of every one of them, whether lost or landed, would have provided a drama unsurpassed on any other river in Britain, such was the turbulence and irregular nature of the Awe's headlong descent.

from *A Salmon-Fisher's Odyssey*
by John Ashley-Cooper, 1982

162

BIG FISH FLY

Trout can be taken at night on all types of flies but the wet fly has produced the most large trout for me. Although I have caught trout tied on hook sizes 6, 8 and 10 most of the flies I use are large. I prefer sizes from 4 to 2/0. My philosophy is, if you are after large trout, use the large flies! Of all the flies I have used, one stands out head and shoulders above the rest. Following is how I came to originate this pattern.

The trout that was slashing and racing all over the riffly water at the head of the long pool I was fishing had refused all the standard wet flies I had previously used for night fishing. My only deduction was that I needed a large fly and I didn't have any. After a frustrating hour of casting, I decided to go home. As soon as I shucked my fishing clothes I headed for the fly tying room and decided to tie a fly big enough to interest the trout I had heard that evening.

I clamped a large 2/0 Allcock hook in the vise and concocted a fly with a short tail, heavy palmered dubbed body plus wings from the breast feathers of a Canadian goose that were tied, one on each side, in front of the hackle so that the concave side faced the eye of the hook. The wing span was over two inches. What a creature! I wondered if I would be able to cast it. I would soon find out.

The next evening after dinner I strung up a heavier rod with a matching line and a short seven-foot leader tapered to ten pounds. To this I tied on the fly. If I connected with that trout I was really going to stick it to him!

Since I had only about a four-mile drive to the stream I did not leave home until the sun started to settle on the horizon. All I could think of was the thrashing and splashing antics of that lunker brown. It seemed a long wait in the car until it was really dark, then I checked all my equipment, locked the car and headed across the meadow to the head of the pool.

I sat down on the bank, made a few casts to see how the fly would react and must admit there was quite a fluttering noise as it whizzed past my ear, but I was satisfied because I could cast it across the stream to the far bank. I reeled in, laid the rod down at my side, and waited for some indication of the lunker starting to feed. I sat there for nearly an hour before I heard a gurgling noise near the far bank. At first I thought it was a muskrat submerging to enter its home but within a few seconds the water erupted in the center of the stream. This was what I was waiting for! Needless to say it didn't take me long to get in position above the trout. I stripped off twenty-five or thirty feet of line and as soon as I located the fish again, I cast above and beyond where I had heard the last splash.

As the fly swung downstream I retrieved with a very slow hand twist and slight tip action. Before I fished out the cast the brown slashed after something almost under my rod tip. The fish was so close, I was afraid of spooking it so I just held the fly motionless in the shallow, riffly water. Without any warning the rod was almost jerked out of my hand and the riffles exploded. The reel screamed as the trout raced to the tail end of the pool where it sulked. As fast as I could take in line, I moved down the bank until I was below the brown and began to apply pressure. The lunker dogged it for a few minutes then headed for the undercut bank on the far side of the pool. With the heavy leader I was using, I pressured the fish back to the shallow tail end of the pool and played him there until he began to flounder in the shallows. I turned on my pencil flashlight, held it in my mouth and pointed the beam on the trout. I said to myself, "What a monster!" Now came the big decision; should I try to beach it or net it? The net looked mighty small but I decided it would be best under existing conditions. Applying all the pressure the rod would take, I eased him over the net and when I scooped he folded in the mesh. When I was thirty feet back from the stream

I dumped out the net and gazed at the largest trout I had ever caught up to that time, a hook-jawed male brown, twenty-six inches long. Since that lunker I have caught hundreds more on the same fly pattern, the largest, a twenty-eight and one-half incher that weighed eight and one-half pounds.

The pattern was so deadly on large brown trout that I kept it a secret for over fifteen years and then only showed it to a few close friends. It will outfish the conventional flies by so large a margin that all who have used this pattern will use no other when night fishing. In fact, the largest brown ever taken in Pennsylvania, a thirty-four inch, fifteen pound five ounce monster was taken on this pattern by my fishing companion, Joe Humphreys, who now teaches the Angling courses I started at Pennsylvania State University in 1934.

Now for the first time I am going to tell all; how to tie and fish the fly that will outfish all other wet fly patterns I have ever used for night fishing.

I believe the effectiveness of this fly is primarily related to the wings. They are tied in such a manner that they "push" water. In the slow moving stretches and pools that hold most of the sizeable browns, this fly will attract trout when most conventional patterns will be ignored. When large browns are cruising at night they sometimes cover a considerable area. In some of the long placid pools they move over a hundred yards or farther, up or down, from the undercut bank, brush pile or daylight holding areas.

As a result one must be patient when covering such water. Personally, I have taken most of the larger fish in two places; the shallow or riffly water at the head of the pool or at the shallow tail end. However, one cannot afford to skip the water between these two areas because you never know where you might hang one of these night feeders.

Generally I start fishing in the riffles at the head of a pool and may stay put in one spot for fifteen or twenty minutes before moving down stream a step or two. In the middle area of the pool I generally move faster, then spend about the same amount of time on the tail end of the pool as I did on the head end. If I know the pool holds a trophy trout I may repeat the above procedure for several hours.

One night, after fishing through a meadow on Spring Creek, I started for the car. I thought I would look over the water with my flashlight. In the riffles at the head of the first pool I spotted a large brown. I snapped off the light, moved above the trout and presented the large wet fly. I held the fly stationary over the fish and he immediately smacked it! I have located more large trout with a flashlight than any other way. Many times when you put the light on a trout it will immediately leave. It is well to remember the next night you will no doubt find the trout in nearly the same place. Of course the spotting of trout is not possible in large rivers and here one must pick the areas he thinks are the best.

When one locates one of the lunker browns, it can usually be taken if one has patience and fishes the water correctly. I should mention, and this is very important, the dark of the moon has produced most all of the large trout for me. In fact, I will not spend much time fishing when the moon is out at night and shining on the water. Sometimes it is possible to take fish before the moon comes up, or in a heavily shaded area, but as a general rule the fishing is usually poor. Only on rare occasions have I had any exceptional luck during this time.

The night fisherman should be thoroughly acquainted with the area he is going to fish. If the stream is small enough to cast across one should know the length of line necessary to reach the far bank. One should know where the trees, bushes and other obstacles are located. Otherwise, one would be hung up most of the time and soon lose interest and probably would spook any trout that was feeding.

When fishing this large night fly, cast across and slightly down stream. If the water is quite sluggish I retrieve with a hand twist and tip action. The retrieve must be slow! In riffly water, where the current gives action to the fly, the retrieve should be very slow, sometimes just holding the fly stationary is very effective. On the shallow flats at the tail end of the pools, retrieve just fast enough to keep the fly from snagging on the bottom. If one follows these suggestions, it will be almost impossible not to catch some fish.

At night you can use a leader heavy enough to handle most large trout. I generally use a tapered leader to ten pound test. I have experimented with all sizes of leaders and never found any significant difference between the lighter and heavier leaders. The heavier leaders allows the angler to set the larger size hook in the tough jaws of a lunker fish and to control the fish after it is hooked.

One thing I know for sure, once you hang a trophy brown at night you will be hooked too!

Harvey's Night Fly

This is the fly that has taken more large trout for me than all other flies combined. I tie the fly on large hooks, sizes 4 to 2/0. Tie in the tail and hackle for ribbing. Dub heavily for the body.

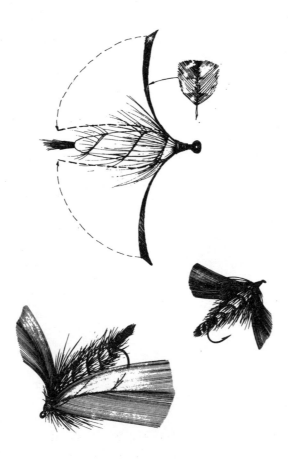

Wind the dubbing up close to the eye but end this body abruptly. This will give you a wedge to help flare out the wings as shown. After palmering is completed, tie in another hackle and wind on tight against the body. Now select two matching, heavily quilled breast feathers. I use goose or duck depending on the size of the hook. Wings should be long enough to reach back to the bend of the hook. I don't believe color makes much difference with the night flies, however, I am a little partial to the darker colors.

Tie the wings so they flare out at the sides.

from *Techniques of Trout-Fishing and Fly-Tying*
© 1990 by George W. Harvey.
Reprinted by permission of
Lyons & Burford, Publishers, New York.

FLOAT-FISHING IN SOUTH AFRICA

The champion shark-fisher of Hermanus, and also, I feel sure, of the whole world, is Mr W.R. Selkirk. I readily grant that his methods of fishing do not allow his fish to be classified as world's records in the usually-accepted sense of the term; but they are the only possible ones to use.

He has caught some twenty-five sharks each of which weighs 1,000 lb or over! His record fish weighed 2,176 lb and measured 13 feet 3 inches in length. Mr Selkirk fought this fish *from the shore for five solid hours*. He is, of course, a very powerful man, but even so the feat is one which requires extraordinary stamina.

Mr Selkirk uses a whole-bamboo rod, large single-action reel, 18-thread line, and, what disqualifies his fish from the record point of view, a large float. This float consists of a four-gallon paraffin tin filled with air under pressure by means of a cycle pump. Unless so "inflated" the tin would collapse under water pressure when the shark dived. This float is secured to the heavy wire trace some 9 feet from the hook, which is baited with a dead fish of 8 lb to 10 lb weight. Mr Selkirk found that the shark's tails often cut his line while being played, so he now employs a second long wire trace between float and reel-line.

Now Mr Selkirk's speciality is man-eating sharks, and he is probably the world's greatest expert at the game. When a shark is seen he baits up and allows his big float to drift out into the bay. When the shark takes hold, the float travels through the water with the wake of a motor-launch! A big shark will totally submerge the float for several minutes at a time; but the buoyancy of the air-filled tin, plus the pull of rod and line soon brings him to the surface again. Frequently a shark attacks the float and the angler then has to reel in line and jerk the float away. The ferocity with which a shark will go for the float must be seen to be believed, and should it obtain a grip with its enormous jaws the tin is instantly punctured. At times, of course, the shark tries to smash the tin flat with his tail, and sometimes succeeds. I have seen Mr Selkirk play a shark in this manner – an 800-pounder, or thereabouts – and at the termination of the struggle the fish was absolutely killed and floating belly upwards; it was then lanced and hauled up the rocks.

Fishing from the rocks as Mr Selkirk does, it is obvious that, unless a float were employed, no tackle on earth would hold these huge man-eaters, and therefore his method is the only possible one to use. On those occasions on which the shark has grabbed the float he has invariably broken the tackle and escaped.

Mr Selkirk uses a ball-bearing reel with no brakes whatsoever; merely a leather hand-pad. He employs a belt with rod bucket and a single shoulder strap.

On one occasion a shark broke the line and was seen towing the float round the bay. The angler embarked in a boat, picked up the trailing line, knotted it on to his reel-line and eventually killed the fish; but not before it had attacked, and nearly upset, the boat!

from *Game Fish Records*
by Jock Scott, 1936

FARAWAY PLACES

FALKLAND FISHING

In March 1992 I was given the opportunity to fish in the Falkland Islands. Since the brief occupation of the islands by the Argentineans and their routing by the Task Force in 1982, it has become relatively easy to visit. The RAF fly twice weekly from the UK, and there is a direct service from Chile.

I had heard stories of tremendous sea trout fishing, and so having some spare time whilst in Chile I flew to Port Stanley from Punta Areanas.

The Falkland Island Tourist Board made all the necessary arrangements, and the following day I was fishing the Warrah River in West Falkland.

The Warrah is a typical West Coast river reminiscent of so many rivers of Ireland and Scotland. Peaty water meandering through moorland plains, deep holding pools, with fast rocky runs between. Foaming rather than rising, from many small tributaries draining the surrounding moor.

My first few casts in one of the deep holding pools to a moving fish, produced an explosive encounter with a nice fresh run fish of six pounds. Plenty more followed, and in the next few days I fished the length of the river, and had caught numerous fish with several over ten pounds. My only company, the native upland Geese and I then travelled to San Carlos in East Falkland, the site of the main Task Force landings to fish the San Carlos River. The river also has beginnings from many small tributaries deep in the heart of the moor, which join to produce the river which is a magnificent sight. Miles of meanders with pools varying in size from a few yards long to several hundred yards. All around twenty-five yards wide. The water is peaty and contains numerous small stunted trout as well as sea trout. I fished from the estuary up and was lucky to catch fish throughout.

I was staying at the new fishing camp run by William and Lynda Anderson, owners of Blue Beach Lodge in San Carlos, and was walking and fishing my way up the river. The camp is placed centrally on the river and allows great accessibility to a lot of good pools.

I set off in the morning and fished upstream of the camp and was enjoying some wonderful fishing, despite the fact that the gale was tipping a mixture of hail and sleet down the back of my neck. However, I was happy as the fish were there and in cooperative mood.

I had planned to map out the pools as I fished up the river, but this proved impossible as the spate was so high, although the water was clean.

Instead I walked up-river and had a cast or two in likely-looking places, and this way I covered a lot of water, and caught a number of fish in the four to eight-pound bracket. At four-thirty I should have turned for home, as I had about five miles of rough country between me and the camp, but I couldn't resist a few more casts in a pool that looked so enticing a few hundred yards further up. I thought I would have a few minutes more before stopping.

The wind had by now reached a full gale and I was having trouble controlling things so I thought I would taper my cast. I had been fishing with a ten-pound cast and a size eight teal blue and silver double. I had some six-pound nylon and stuck that on.

My next and final cast in a likely-looking spot seemed a little better, and as the fly swung round in the current it stopped. "Rock" I cursed, and pulled to free it. Suddenly the water boiled and a huge shape hurled itself out of the river, landing with a crash and spray of water. I had seen some big fish in the past few weeks, but not like this.

It hurled itself around the pool, and spent an alarming amount of time in the air, and all I could do was try and stay near it. Mindful of the light tippet I was unable to do much about it. For two interminable hours it raced around the river, leaving the pool to run upstream, then changing its mind and coming back down like a charging buffalo, only to sulk under a shelf and grate the line on a rock, and refuse to budge. It then changed tactics and roared off downstream whilst I desperately removed as much clothing as possible on the run, in preparation for the inevitable soaking. Half a lifetime later and a mile downstream it was pretty tired: I was exhausted, terrified and soaked. However, it wasn't over yet.

I had no net and each time I edged the fish in to the bank, it would turn its head away and the current would sweep it away down the river. This went on until in desperation I waded out into the stream, knelt down and scooped it up across my knees. I stayed there, terrified to move, as one slip would mean disaster whilst I tried to make a plan. Eventually, by dropping my rod and scuttling crab-like with the fish locked in a vice-like grip I made it to the safety of the bank. Having spent the past two hours sure that it was going to end in tears, I couldn't believe the sight before my eyes. I had never seen such a fish, a real fish of a lifetime. It was huge. Then reaction set in, the shaking could have been because of the weather and my advanced state of undress, but the silly smirk and the euphoria shared only with some rather startled geese was definitely because of the beautiful silver fish in front of me.

By now it was almost dark, and my bag and coat and sundry items of clothing were strewn about for a mile upstream. It was time to go. Having collected it all together and fitted some of the fish into my bag I set off on the long trek back to camp, eventually arriving with what felt like a marlin on my back.

Two days later in Port Stanley when the fish was finally weighed, at twenty-two pounds twelve and a half ounces, I was still euphoric. Two moments will live with me for the rest of my life. The first time I saw that fish, and the look on William Anderson's face when he came to collect me and first saw my passenger!

Alison Faulkner

"Bet You Can't"

Once again I had returned across the Magellan Straits to Tierra del Fuego to stay with the de las Carreras family at Kan Tapen (the Indian name for Fishing House). Their son Fernando was now organising the fishing on the Rio Grande, which runs through their estanzia.

It was into the Rio Grande, one hundred miles north of Cape Horn, that John Godall, the English manager of the family's meat-packing station, had put the first parr. He hatched them from the brown trout he had so hopefully imported. Before that, so 86-year-old Bill Waldron told me, there were only what he called "mud trout", six or seven inches long, in the river: at least, that was all he ever caught. He helped John Godall to stock the Rio Grande and other rivers on the island with these parr. The fish grew fast, feeding voraciously I am sure on the many crustacea I could see in the river. Then, like our salmon, they went out to sea to feed and grow, returning to spawn in their own rivers.

Perhaps it was the happy memory of the endless games of "I bet you can't" that my sister and I used to play, that made me take up Fernando's ridiculous challenges. I had told him how it had taken me four years to achieve the dream I set myself before my first trip to South America. It was to see a condor in the sky and to have a sea trout on my line at the same time. The first year, on the Serrano river in remote southern Chile, there was a magnificent condor floating in the sky. But when I had my only

176

sea trout of the day on my line, he had gone. Three years later, on the Rio Grande, sea trout and condor were there together at last. Fernando thought this was both amusing and ridiculous and said he would give me some more challenges for the two weeks I was fishing on the river. So started the most extraordinary weeks' fishing I have ever had, or am likely to have. This was my fourth visit to what Ferdinand Magellan called the Land of Fire when he saw it across the straits in 1520. I believe it must have been a combination of the warning fires lit by the Indians when they first saw his ship, and the overwhelming wonderful orange-red sunsets that made him believe the whole land was on fire. It is an extraordinary place, quite different from anywhere else. Some people don't like it. I have known fishermen leave after two days; they can't stand the wind and weather. For me there is an extraordinary atmosphere about this land. I get an extra feeling of adventure and excitement there and nothing seems quite real. There is, I am sure, more sky down there than land, and just knowing the next place is the South Pole, makes the words "uttermost part of the earth" seem true.

My week started with the near-impossible happening. Due to a storm and late departure, my plane had flown to Montreal instead of Buenos Aires! So, if anyone had then said, "Bet you can't arrive on time at Rio Grande", I should definitely have agreed with them. I should have realised then, when I landed almost dead on time, after two nights and a day in the air, that something pretty amazing was being set in motion.

The weather in Tierra del Fuego was much better than usual; no roaring wind, and a blue sky. The river was at a perfect height and clear. This year the wildlife seemed to have gathered close together on the Pampas – on my first evening I saw flamingo, beaver, guanaco, duck, fox and geese, and the gleaming silver jumping sea trout. I was in love with the place again.

The first jokey, "bet you can't" challenge, was for me to catch a new weight record of 500 pounds in a week, for the lodge. I really thought it was totally impossible, even with perfect conditions. After two days I could see I had a chance. There was a run of big fish in the river. Like salmon, the big ones seem to come into the river together, and stay together, like families and friends.

What a week I had! The fish loved me, my casting got better and better, and the usual terrible south-westerly wind blew less.

I seemed to have been given boundless energy, and every fishing spirit there ever was, was beside me. At the end of the week I'd done it. What luck I had had, and what wonderful days! It would never ever happen to me in my life again, I knew that. I don't think I would ever want it to.

The next challenge was just farcical. I was to have a fish on my line, with a guanaco looking at me. Laughingly, I felt I had to say, "Of course I can". Fernando, the guide and I all knew that it was really just about impossible. The guanaco is rather a shy creature and stays well away from the river. You can see them, some days, in small groups out on the pampas. To me they look like a cross between a llama and a deer, with beautiful soft ginger fur. Besides their meat, it was also for their fur that they were shot and hunted to near extinction. Now they are protected. When I saw, and felt a guanaco fur rug in a shop for the first time, I realised that it was a guanaco rug I had been sick on in the back of the Rolls as a child! Now this strange creature was somehow to come near me – impossible. It was a one in a million chance for one even to be near the river, let alone stay and wait for a fish.

At every pool, I looked around for a guanaco; of course there never was one. The wind suddenly got up, and I certainly was not thinking about guanacos any more, as head down, I battled against the blast for a long walk to the last pool. We had to wade the icy river and John Ryan, my guide, sensibly got hold of my belt, so I would not be swept away (the water was nearly up to my waist). So, thinking of survival rather than of guanacos, we arrived at the last pool. It was called Lilla's Pool, after me, because two years ago I had caught the first fish in it when it was only a small dull pool and a long walk. Now, after the winter storms, it was unrecognisable. A beautiful large deep pool, and there, standing on the opposite bank, was a big male guanaco looking haughtily at me, with his head held high on his long neck. We were both rooted to the ground in amazement. A guanaco waiting for me, at my pool – the sheer impossibility of it gave me an eerie feeling, and I now knew that somehow I would also get a fish. So, very quietly and confidently, I fished down my pool – no false casts, no jumpy movements, and he was still looking at me. Suddenly, I saw the funny and ridiculous side to all this and I started to laugh quietly with excitement. I gave the guanaco a wink, and in the middle of the pool, my heart beating fast, I felt the thrilling tug I had been waiting for. A

178

big jump, a noisy splash – but the fish was still on, the guanaco still staring at me. It had happened – when we finally landed the lovely 18-pound fish, the guanaco had gone. So, it was a jubilant return to the lodge. They hardly believed us, so I was glad to have had a witness.

Now, with two days left, I was longing to hear what the last "bet you can't" would be. This time the challenge was not so totally impossible – I was to have a sea trout on my line, and a beaver swimming across the river at the same time. Again, it was a matter of pure luck. There certainly were more beavers in the river than guanacos on the bank, but to get the combination right, I would certainly, once again need to have the fishing spirits on my side!

Downstream, on the wider part of the river, the wind had dropped. It was nearly nine o'clock in the evening, the magic sunset hour. Nearly every evening at this time, the terrible wind dropped, the magical silence broken only by the honking and swishing wings of the low-flying Magellan's Upland geese. They were returning to their roosting grounds on the stony islands in the river. It was, as always, a magical and beautiful time. The glowing sky was reflected in the still river, and now and again a silver fish would jump and splash. I had to stop and wonder at it all. Suddenly I saw a beaver swimming head high across the river. Even to see him made me smile – I was halfway there with the challenge, and that, I thought, was a lucky omen. I gave him a wave, and started to fish. Some minutes later, a small fish took my no.6 G.P. I was concentrating hard on this lively silver jumper, when Jonas shouted out to me, "A beaver, Lilla, a beaver!" and there he was, swimming steadily back to his beaver house. My fish was still on the line!

My prize was an exciting flight in a tiny plane across the Magellan Straits to Punta Arenas in Chile. Fernando took me to see the house where his fearless great-grandparents had lived, now an interesting museum. Here we ate delicious centolla crab, and laughed about the incredible weeks.

Near the house is the plaza de Arinas. In the middle of this square stands the huge and impressive statue of Ferdinand Magellan. There is also, at the side of this statue, a figure of a Fuegian Indian. Legend says that if you kiss his well worn and now shiny toe, you will return. As I bent to touch and kiss the toe, I did not say a wish to return, but said a near-tearful thank you to the magical Indians, who by their affinity with nature and animals must surely have been playing games with me on the river.

Footnote: Number and weight of sea trout caught between 27 January and 2 February 1990 on the Rio Grande in Tierra del Fuego, staying at Kan Tapen:

56 sea trout, average weight 11 lbs

Total weight 604 lbs including four fish between 19 and 21 lbs.

"This is a record for our lodge over the last six years."
(*signed*) Fernando M. de las Carreras

Lilla Rowcliffe

The Anniversary

The Skjerna is a small river in Jutland, scarcely known outside a narrow circle of Danish anglers. Here, at Easter 1954, Copenhagen tobacconist Dinesen hooked the salmon of a lifetime.

It is now exactly 25 years since I lost my soul to the Skjerna, and one might say that I celebrated the anniversary as no one had ever celebrated before . . .

Like many others before me, I started my fishing career with an old hazel stick, a piece of string and a penny hook, or was it five pence a dozen, I don't remember.

My quarry were mainly roach and other whitefish, but soon I moved on to perch and in due course, pike. After years of fishing, I considered myself capable of trying for the mightiest of them all, the salmon.

So it happened that I cast my line in the Skjerna at Easter exactly 25 years ago for the first time. The reason for my losing my soul was that by beginner's luck I was granted a 32-pounder the first year, a magnificent fish, a bit large for a beginner, but again I considered myself lucky.

Despite the fact that luck seemed to abandon me after that, I kept on returning to the river year after year, always at Easter. I had been captured not only by the fish but by the river itself and by the secluded beauty of the windswept land, so different from Copenhagen where I lived. Yes, the Skjerna remained the target every year, despite the long intervals between salmon being landed.

After the 32-pounder, 12 years passed before I caught my second salmon, a 20-pounder, and then a further five years before another, a fine fish of 26 pounds. Then followed seven blank years until the spring of 1954, the Easter that gave me the adventure of my life.

Many stories have been told about that day. Now I feel the urge to relieve my heart by telling what really happened.

When we drove off from Copenhagen my wife, who incidentally is also a very keen fisher, said to me, "If you catch a salmon this year, you could really call it an anniversary salmon." Thank God, she did not know at the time that those were prophetic words.

On Maundy Thursday we started fishing the "Highway Curve", as it is called, because of its characteristic bend and mirror-like flow. We fished all morning. It was freezing cold with a harsh westerly wind, the water running well above average height, perhaps not the best day for fishing.

We shivered and our thoughts soon turned to the warm cozy fire and well stocked table at the Skjern inn, no more than a few miles down river. But I remembered the tough words of an old Jutlander I once knew: "T'catch yer salmon, y'll keep yer spoon well in the water!" And so we stuck at it, finished our lunch quickly and continued fishing the "Cattle crossing". My wife and my fishing mate were already in action before I had rigged my rod and was able to start, so I wandered off downstream, but alas, this place was already taken.

The river narrows a bit here, the current is deep and strong, an ideal place for salmon according to previous experience, so there was little to do but wait my turn. This was the place I wanted to fish.

The other fishing party was now at a fair distance downstream, I was ready to start. My tackle – a light eight foot spinning rod of English make purchased 22 years before was my trusted friend and had caught me many salmon, a Pflueger Supreme multiplier with a 35-pound test line rigged with a one-ounce Devon were the tools that would soon show their mettle.

I must have cast three or four times when I suddenly spotted a veritable tidal wave some 20 feet behind my Devon, and before I could react and get my thoughts together I felt a violent jerk that jarred me to the bone and seconds later a gigantic beast jumped clean out of the water.

I was shocked. My arms and legs started trembling; never had I seen such a salmon before.

My rod was bent like a cheese-cutter and the reel screamed as the beast rushed downstream. It jumped again, a mighty leap that revealed a salmon in all its silvery armour. "I will never get this fish," I thought, "it is a Troll!"

Soon the others joined me, and slowly my nerves steadied. I didn't have much control of the fish, she was sovereign ruler here. I just had to follow as well as I could.

Now the fish didn't show itself but fought deep and swam steadily downstream which presented a potential hazard as a small cluster of tall bushes blocked the bank some 200 yards below. It would be impossible for me to pass them with my short rod, and I suddenly realised that the end was near. But luck was with us. A local salmon fisherman of great experience, Mr Gaardsvig, the house-painter, hacked off the tops of the bushes and we managed to raise the line over the remaining stubs.

The salmon ran on, steadily driving us downstream another 400 and 500 yards with no sign of weakening until the next hazard appeared. The marshy flooded meadow ahead was only passable in dry conditions, so this would be the end of the road. Now she would show what she was made of! I decided to put rod and line to the test.

Another local fisherman, Mr Kolding, the blacksmith from Troldhede village, was the only one in possession of a long gaff. It was agreed that he should attempt to land her. I tried to draw the fish towards the bank and almost succeeded a couple of times, but each time she saw us and immediately headed out again. She was strong and seemed very much aware of her capabilities and we soon realised that there might still be far to go before she was tired.

We chose another tactic. Once more I applied as much pressure on my Farlow rod as it could take until the fish was some three feet from the bank – what an unbelievably strong rod! It was incredible that it held. The smith then crawled up from behind like a Red Indian and took her by surprise. A quick slash with the gaff, a gigantic splash from her shovel of a tail and there she was suddenly, 10 feet up in the grass. Silence followed. It seemed like hours before someone whispered: "This is impossible!"

We carried the salmon to the car. It had to be weighed quickly as we thought the old record might be close to being beaten. It was! The scale stopped at an incredible 58 pounds. The length was 55 inches and the girth 31 inches. It was a dream come true; just once in my life to catch a fish of such a size that I never have to lie to my friends!

From the official records:
Mr Dinesen's salmon was later officially examined and found to be six years old. It had spent two years in the river before entering the sea as a smolt, where it had then spent four years. It was a hen fish on her first spawning run. She had gained an amazing 13 pounds per sea year, a true queen of the river.

Translated by Henrik Strandgaard of Copenhagen from the original article in Jaeger & Fisker magazine.

Footnote: According to his friends, Mr Dinesen was never the same again. After the capture of his great fish he went into a gradual decline, finally taking to his bed. In an attempt to revive his spirits, his friends and family placed a cast of the Skjerna salmon in his bedroom, fixed to the wall. Unfortunately this did not produce the hoped-for rally, and the tobacconist soon faded away.

STRANGE GOINGS-ON

It Came as a Big Surprise

Byron Rogers

There is an Angler's Prayer you still come across occasionally, painted on old mugs in fishing inns. It is a bit like a river itself, the couplet meandering towards a tired rhyme.

> Lord, grant that I may catch a fish so big that even I,
> When speaking of it afterwards, may have no need to lie.

This is an account of a man, "an excellent angler, and now with God," as Walton put it, who did just that. He caught a fish so big it would have needed two large men, their arms fully outstretched, to give cynics in saloon bars even a hint of its dimensions.

But he did more than that. He went fishing for salmon one day and caught something so peculiar, so far removed from even the footnotes of angling in Britain, that a grown man who was present ran off across the fields. Nobody would have thought it at all odd that day if the fisherman had been found trying to look up his catch in the Book of Revelations.

It needs a photograph. The fisherman is dead. His friends are beginning to die. If a photograph had not been taken few people would now believe what happened. A hundred years ago, ballads and hearsay would have wrecked it on the wilder shores of myth. As it is yellowing cuttings from the local paper, almost crumbling into carbon, are slowly unfolded from wallets. A print is unearthed reverently from under a pile of household receipts. It was on July 28, 1933, that Alec Allen caught his fish, but even that has been elbowed into myth. His obituary (far from the national press) says that it was on July 9. The *Guinness Book of Records* says that it was July 25. But the one contemporary cutting had no doubts. It was July 28. Appropriately it was a Friday.

The photograph is extraordinary. Allen, a short man in a Fairisle pullover and baggy trousers, leans against a wall beside a trestle. It is a typical Thirties snapshot slouch. His hands are in his pockets. There is a cigarette in his mouth. But of course you notice all this a long time afterwards, because of the thing dangling from the trestle.

At first it looks like the biggest herring in the history of the sea. It towers over the man by a good four feet. It is a fish certainly, but the head ends in a dark snout. The body appears to be armoured. The surroundings, a farm gate, the field beyond, underline the oddness. In a farmyard a man is posing beside a thing the size of a basking shark. Alec Allen had caught himself a Royal Sturgeon in the River Towy, at Nantgaredig, near Carmarthen. It was nine feet two inches long, had a girth of 59 inches, and weighed 388 pounds.

Allen was a commercial traveller from Penarth in Glamorganshire. He was a well-known sportsman and hockey referee. In later life he was to referee Olympic matches. But he was then in his early forties, one of that oddly innocent breed who figure in Saki and Wodehouse, but who latterly seem to have become as extinct as the Great Auk, the sporting bachelor. His great delight was fishing, but in him it was more than a delight.

His great friend was Alderman David Price of Nantgaredig, who died last year aged 74. He had known Allen all his life. All they had ever talked about, he recalled with wonder, was fishing.

In 1933 Allen was traveller for a firm of fishing tackle manufacturers. His father, also a great fisherman, was a traveller for a wallpaper firm. Father and son somehow contrived it that they could travel together in the same car. Both their commercial beats were West Wales, but a West Wales wonderfully concentrated between the rivers Wye, Teify and Towy. When their friends talk about the Allens it is with amusement. It was notorious that their business rounds were engineered for fishing.

Off-stage Hitler was ranting. Stalin drawing up lists of

victims. Ramsay MacDonald droned his platitudes and the dole queues lengthened. But in West Wales the Allens went their way, in a car full of tackle and wallpaper, their itineraries perfectly arranged to end in fishing inns beside rivers. The thing has an idyllic quality. It may have been a bit tough on you if your wallpaper shop was nowhere near a river, but nobody seems to have complained. In time the son succeeded the father as wallpaper salesman, but the itineraries did not change.

The two had rented a stretch of the Towy since 1928. This included some of the deepest pools in the river. But the summer of 1933 had been dry, and the water level was low. Walking by one of the pools that July, Alec Allen noted enormous waves suddenly cross it. It puzzled him but at the time he would have discounted any suspicion that they had been made by a living thing. After all, it was 15 miles to the sea, and tidal water ended two miles lower down.

A few days later Allen returned to the pool. It was evening and he had a friend with him, Edwin Lewis of Crosshands. There was a third man, his name lost to history, watching on the bank. Allen began fishing. It was a quiet evening. But then he felt a slight tug on his line. He pulled on it but to no effect.

Alderman Price was fond of telling what happened next. "Alec used to tell me that he thought he'd hooked a log. He couldn't see what it was, except that it was something huge in the shadows. Then the log began to move upstream." A faint smile would come over Price's face.

"Now Alec knew that logs don't move upstream."

Allen had still no idea of what was in the river. A more imaginative man might have become frightened at that stage. His line was jerking out under a momentum he had never experienced. In the darkness of the pool he had hooked something which moved with the force of a shark.

He played it for 20 minutes, letting the line move out when it went away. When it came back he retreated up the bank. But there was no channel of deep water leading away from the pool. If there had been, no salmon line made would have held his catch. Then he saw it.

Suddenly the creature leapt out of the water. Maddened, it crashed into a shallow run. It was there under them, threshing in the low water. Allen was confronted by a bulk that was just not possible. The sightseer ran shouting for his life.

But Lewis ran forward with the gaff. He stuck it into the fish, but the fish moved. It straightened the steel gaff. Then the great tail flicked up and caught Lewis, and threw him into the air on to the bank. Just one flick, but it nearly broke the man's leg.

There was a large rock on the bank. Allen dropped the rod (it had been a freak catch, the hook snagging in the fish's head, a sturgeon having no mouth) and tugged at the rock. With it in his hands he waded out, and dropped it on the head, lifting it again and pounding at it. The creature began to die. The two men looked down at it. Neither had any idea what it was.

But in death it provided them with an even greater problem; how were they to get it out of the river? Allen ran to a nearby farm. There then occurred one of those rare moments which cannot help but be pure comedy. Allen asked could he borrow a horse and cart. The farmer, naturally, asked why. Allen said he had caught a fish.

It ended with farmer, farmer's friends, dogs, horse, cart and all going back to the bank.

"I can remember it now," said Alderman Price. "Alec came running to my house. I had never seen him so excited. All he would say was, 'Well, I've caught something this time that you'll never beat.' I went back with him. They'd pulled it up on to the trestle you see in the photographs and the news had got round. People were coming in cars and in carts. They were ferrying children across the river.

"It had these big scales, I remember. Very slimy. It was a sort of black and white in colour. No, I wasn't frightened." He was in the habit of pausing at that point. "It was dead."

As the anglers gathered it was determined that the thing out of the river was a sturgeon. Vague memories stirred. Was it not the law that a sturgeon was the King's prerogative?

A telegram was sent to Buckingham Palace inquiring after the King the next day. A stiff little reply came the same day, that the King was not in residence. Such trivia did not deter a man who had hooked the biggest fish in recorded angling history. Allen sold the sturgeon to a fishmonger from Swansea for two pounds ten shillings.

That worked out at something like a penny ha'penny a pound and this at a time when Scotch salmon at Billingsgate was fetching two and six a pound. More than 40 years later Allen's friends who had helped him load the thing on to the train, were still bitter about the deal.

There had been so much caviar in the sturgeon that some of it had fallen on to the farm yard where it was eaten by those of the farmer's pigs with a taste for the good life. History does not relate what happened to the pigs subsequently. But selling the fish did get rid of one problem. There were no refrigerators in the Valley, and 388 pounds of sturgeon was a lot of fish.

Allen fished on until his death in 1972 at the age of 77. In photographs the lean figure became stocky. Spectacles were added. Catches got held up regularly to the camera, something he could never have done that wild July night when he was content just to pose beside his fish. So did he consider the rest of his fishing life to be a sort of epilogue?

Brian Rudge, who now runs the fishing tackle firm on whose behalf Allen meandered through West Wales, knew him well. "I think he saw the incident as more of a joke than anything. He wasn't a man who was easily impressed. I think, you know, that as far as he was concerned it was a bit of a nuisance. He was out salmon fishing. The sturgeon had got in his way."

Alderman Price heard Allen talk about it a few times. "It was usually when he heard anglers going on about their catches. He wasn't a boasting man but sometimes he couldn't resist saying, 'Well, I suppose this would be the biggest fish I ever caught.' And then of course they'd say, 'Good God.'"

Yet outside the valley and angling circles it was a small fame. There was no mention of it in the national press that July.

It was a small item even in the *Carmarthen Journal*. The august organ rose to its greatest heights of sensationalism. "Two anglers had an exciting time while fishing in the River Towy," the report began.

In March, 1972, Allen died suddenly at the home in Penarth he had shared with a spinster sister. But there was a passage in his will which surprised his friends almost as much as the catching of the sturgeon. Though he had talked little about the incident, he left instructions that his body be cremated and the ashes put into the river at the spot out of which he had pulled Leviathan.

"I called on David Price one day," said Ronald Jones, the former Chief Constable of Dyfed, and another of Allen's friends, "and said what a pity it was about Alec." "Aye," said Dai. "I've got him there on the mantelpiece." It was the casket, you see.

We were all surprised. Nobody's ever heard of anyone wanting that done before."

"I suppose it was a romantic touch," said Brian Rudge, "but he wasn't the sort of man who'd like people to gather round a grave."

It was a grey wet day when they put the ashes into the water. A dozen of his old friends, contacted by phone or letter, gathered on the bank. No clergyman or minister had agreed to take part, their religion not recognising a river as consecrated ground.

Despite the hymns in the rain, it would seem to have had pagan overtones. Among the first things a people names are rivers. River gods are the oldest. A man who had pulled out of a river its largest living thing would seem to be assuaging something very old in having himself put back in its place.

"We said the Lord's Prayer," said the Chief Constable, "as we committed the ashes to the waters he'd fished for 50 years. But then as the wind carried them I saw a trout leap into the air just where they were drifting.

"And I said to Dai: 'Look. Alec's there.'"

from *The Sunday Telegraph*

TRICKS OF THE TRADE

Once upon a time – but this is no fairy tale – there lurked within the deeps of a millpool, in the course of a small tributary of the river Tweed, a great trout. The presence of this fish, a monster for that particular little river, had been known for many years, and all the local "experts" had sought its capture by every legitimate – and, it is to be feared, not so legitimate – method. But this big trout would look neither at fly nor worm, be the stream in flood or low and clear. Twice within local memory the fish had been hooked with the aid of a small spinning minnow but on each occasion had simply plunged furiously towards his holt somewhere amid the old wooden piles which flanked one side of the pool and there snapped the taut gut like a cotton thread.

Many a time, when the village anglers were gathered together over their evening ale, the talk would revert to this trout, which gradually assumed a place of importance as one of the local features, at least in the minds of the village piscators. Many a cunning campaign was laid for the great trout's capture, the schemers being spurred on as much by the knowledge of the kudos which would follow success as by tantalizing visions of the fish's vast form adorning the parlour wall. All to no avail, however, were ingenious and subtle plans made and tried, and the great trout lived on to play the tyrant within his deep domain. Short of being finished off by poison or dynamite, which not even the worst poacher in the village would have dared to try on this particular trout, the fish seemed destined to die a natural death.

There came, one spring, to the little Border village a stranger, a man from the South Country, a quiet-spoken individual, distinguished only by the fact that he carried with him a fishing rod. He put up at the village inn, and it was not long ere he learned of the presence of the coveted millpool trout. Slyly, as is often rural wont, the old local anglers suggested that the visitor might have a try for the "muckle troot" before he left, and to this the stranger mildly agreed, apparently unaware of the sardonic twitching of lips and flickering side-glances of amusement which greeted his acceptance of the challenge. And there the matter was left for the time being.

The following day the stranger, minus fishing rod, was observed to visit the millpool. His movements were closely observed, but he did little else but sit whiffing gently at his pipe for almost the entire afternoon. And he repeated the identical tactics for the whole of the following morning, responding to dry banter only with a smile and a shake of the head. Nor did he fish that afternoon, preferring apparently to take his exercise along the quiet country roads and lanes. The old village Izaak Waltons nodded among themselves and observed drily that the stranger might just as well occupy his time with such rural perambulations as try to capture the famous trout. Indeed, apart from being the object of a little good-natured chaff, it was generally conceded that the visitor was a man of sound sense, in so far as he seemed to recognize the impossible when he saw it.

That same evening after supper, the visitor, again without fishing rod or any form of gear, went out for a stroll in the early spring dusk. He went unobserved on this occasion since there were thirsts other than curiosity to be slaked at that time of the day. He was gone only for half an hour or so, then he returned to the inn, joined in a convivial glass of ale and finally retired early to bed.

The next morning, however, the quiet guest was up and about almost before the sleepy-eyed maids had bestirred themselves, and, his fishing rod under his arm, went out into the grey morning. An hour and a half later he returned, bearing with him a huge trout which dipped the scales at 7½ lb. The guest asked his stunned host for an ashet, and having placed the great fish on it, quietly went in to his breakfast.

The news spread like wildfire throughout the angling fraternity in that sleepy little Border village, and men fidgeted throughout their working hours, tantalized by the desire to see for themselves if rumour was true. That evening mine host's comfortable inn did a roaring trade in the way of liquid refreshments. Local anglers, to the accompaniment of many strange and peculiar epithets, looked upon that noble quarry with very mixed feelings of envy, admiration, and something of regret – regret that their famous trout had at last succumbed. But such sentiments did not long endure, and were replaced by intense curiosity and a burning desire to know how it had been done. The stranger, however, would not speak, and resisted the most cunning attempts to extract information.

He departed on his way the following morning, but before he took leave he not only presented his host with the trout but admitted that, as a coarse fisher, it was the first trout he had ever captured, and that, on the whole, he preferred *pike fishing*!

How was it done? The angler, who up to the time of his death was a personal friend of mine, admitted that, because of chance observation, the whole thing was a fluke. While sitting on the bank of the pool he had seen a nestling tumble from a nest among the willows on the other bank. The little bird had scarcely fallen on the water when a great pair of jaws engulfed it. That gave the witness an idea and by spending many hours exploring the hedgerows he managed to find the carcass of a fledgling bird. After mounting this to a large single bait-hook, he took a length of fairly heavy gut-substitute, one end of which he attached to the baited hook; he then contrived to place the unusual bait at the end of a willow shoot in the gathering dusk, lightly hooking the soft green wood with the hook itself. Finally he attached the other end of the length of gut-substitute to a small stone, which he flung right across the pool to the other bank. After this he returned to the inn.

Early the following morning he took his rod, found the gut-substitute, attached it to his reel-line and, having studied positions, etc., twitched the baited hook from its hold on the willow. The rest of the story is obvious. The great trout rose as before, took down the strange bait, was hooked and finally mastered. Though the confessor of this incident persistently sought to discount his performance, it yet remains a notable example of what can be accomplished with observation, intelligence, and, of course, a little luck.

from *Big Trout*
by William H. Lawrie 1955

THE BIG GED

Wen I was a child I was told of a ged that, carried on its captor's shoulder, trailed at his heels as he went triumphantly back with his catch to show it to his master. A ged, I hasten to explain, took its name from the ox goad, a round-ended pole with which a teamster encouraged his animals to haul a wagon uphill. I didn't know a ged was a pike until I grew up.

The man who caught the legendary Loch Ken pike was a gamekeeper, like the man who looked after the moss where my grandfather cut peats and took us for picnics on summer days. There was nothing about fish or fowl that Willie didn't know. Like Esau, he was a man of the fields. It was Willie who provided the long-eared owl that adorned my grandmother's sitting-room until the glass case got broken and the stuffed bird was cremated, appropriately, on a peat fire. Willie often talked about big geds in remote moorland lochs and others in the river that wound its way through the watermeadows we could see from the farm. He knew their ways and how to catch them.

I remember taking his advice and going to catch one of these giants on a long length of binder twine, a bit of red rag and a strip of bacon rind. This hookless device worked so long as the rag didn't tear out of the ged's mouth. Pollution in the river was unknown. It flowed through swaying green weed and dancing water-lilies and was the same colour as good malt whisky. The thing about a ged is that its eyes never close. It just lies there waiting for a foolish fish to come within striking distance. Like the goshawk, it doesn't go in for a long chase. When after a short dash it fails to secure its victim it settles to wait for another. Willie taught me all the ways to get a ged because he was first and foremost a keeper. In those unenlightened days anything that threatened game, fish or fowl, had to be destroyed. No-one ate the ged. It was put out for the hens to devour, which they did with the enthusiasm of vultures. Anything that was left was cleared-up by scavenging pigs.

To return to Willie however, he found himself another job while I was growing up, getting married and raising a family. He moved from the moor where he had kept bees and harvested heather honey, to an estate that owned a good part of the fishing on the river, and lived in a bothy. There he kept an eye on would-be poachers and local characters with a penchant for helping themselves to other people's property. He sat in the bothy on wet days, fashioning flies and spoons and similar lures for salmon and geds. By the time my family reached adolescence I was living a long way from my boyhood haunts and it was natural that I wanted to show them a world I had known so well.

We had a summer holiday in Galloway and I took my rods, hoping to fish waters I had so often fished as a boy. The owner of the small hotel in which we stayed said I must go down and find the keeper. He mentioned the name Willie but everyone in that part of the world seems to be called Willie. Being sent to the bothy just below the stone bridge didn't make me think of Willie Skimming but when I looked in there he was! The years rolled back. He looked keenly at me. "How are you, boy? You haven't come for a salmon, have you?" I had come at the wrong time. The river was low. Fish weren't moving. If anything took a lure it would be one of those old geds, perhaps even one I had tried to catch or looked at on a long-ago summer's day. On such days geds rested in laybys, their green and gold bodies and snouts becoming dusted with fine silt. These big geds were still there until later when the countryside was divided and sub-divided by new highways bringing hundreds of tourists in cars and caravans. The cars deposited oil that washed into the river and pollution spread everywhere.

I had happened to arrive on the day when Willie had caught the biggest ged he had taken from the river in twenty or thirty years. It was there for me to see, lying on a bed of fern at the back of the bothy. I can't remember what weight Willie said it was, but it was a real monster and well into double figures, a very big ged from any river. How had he taken it? It seemed only after having been broken many times with hooks straightened. The great fish had been master of the pool on Willie's very doorstep. No grilse went up without being slashed or left for the gulls to devour as it drifted back downstream dying. A mallard with her brood was hounded across the pool again and again until there was no brood to follow the poor bird. Willie's boss was furious to see so many ducks being taken and told Willie he must get this ged or his job would be on the line. Something stronger than ordinary tackle was certainly called for. Willie fashioned a trace from picture wire and got the blacksmith to forge him a hook that would have done for a shark. His labrador had had a litter of pups and one had died. What better offering for the big ged than a labrador pup? Willie set it all up, tying the line to a tree on the bank and leaving the baited hook in the water overnight. The big ged took the bait and the monster was there in the morning, "moored like a big green submarine". It looked balefully at its captor as he reached for his blackthorn, well-weighted priest. There was a bit of a tussle. The priest rose and fell and rose and fell again. Willie had to put a lot of wood on the fire after he had carried the dead fish into the bothy, and strip to the buff to dry his clothes, for he had had to go in and battle with the fish in its own element. His boss would be well pleased, he said. He was greatly pleased himself and we had a wee dram to celebrate. The monster was the kind of shovel-nosed ged that could frighten a man, even when it was dead, and I don't think I have ever seen a better specimen.

Ian Niall

RIVER SHIN

Many years ago when I was still in my late teens, I was asked over to have a day on the Shin by an old friend of my father's. It was late March and the weather blustery with showers of snow even on the low ground. As the old saying says, the weather was keeping up its reputation by going out in March like a lion.

In those days this river had a strong spring run with many heavy fish amongst them. There was always a chance, therefore, of getting a really big one of 30 lbs or more. Needless to say I looked forward to my day tremendously and as my father's beat of the Cassley had been fishing well recently, I had every hope of getting a fish regardless of size.

When I arrived I was met by the ghillie, Tom, because the head ghillie, Jimmy Macrae, was with another guest. He had already left for the river as they were fishing the Falls beat further upstream. Tommy was not too enthusiastic because he thought that the river had risen overnight and might still be rising for a while yet. Certainly not the best conditions for fly fishing, but hopefully it might settle in the afternoon. They had caught a few fish earlier in the week, but had risen many more that would not come again, and he thought it was probably because the fish were unsettled.

We started off at the Bridge Pool above the road bridge, and then moved on downstream to the Home Pool, below the bridge, a famed pool which could be fished from either side for much of its length when the water level was right.

Tommy had high hopes of catching a fish from one side or the other. However, it was not to be and in spite of trying several favourite flies I only moved one fish right at the tail of the pool from the right bank, and this rose shyly to the fly and never touched. Tommy checked the gauge whilst I was still fishing and told me the river had risen a further three inches since we started and it was still rising at lunchtime.

After having a quick bite to eat, he decided we should try some pools higher upstream and then return to the Home Pool for a last fling before dark. Having fished Smith's and several other pools above it, we eventually reached Black Stone, a small deep glide below the Little Falls. This pool had a great reputation and as we fished it, Tommy recounted numerous stories of big fish that had been taken there and many more of fish that had been lost. By this time the river seemed to have stopped rising and was just holding. After looking at his watch he said, "We will give it one more try and then go back to the Home Pool." Looking in his box he produced a 9/0 Red Sandy with a much heavier iron than those that I had been fishing with and advised me to try it, but to fish it slowly and deep.

I started with a short line at the head of the pool and about my fifth cast, felt my line stop and struck immediately to be met with a firm resistance, but no movement. For a moment I thought I was snagged, but then I felt a slight quiver and knew it was a fish. Tommy was delighted and immediately said, "I think it's a good one." The fish sailed about the pool very quietly, shaking its head, and I knew by the weight that Tommy was probably right. Then after a few minutes the fish just put his head down and began to sulk, barely moving from the same spot. Tommy was puffing away at his pipe and giving me reassuring words of advice, but having been brought up on the Welsh Dee I was well used to big fish and how to handle a sulker. However, having tried all the tricks of the trade, such as heavy side strain to tilt the fish off balance and trying to walk him upstream as well as all the tips that Tommy could think of, it was to no avail. I seriously began to wonder whether I was now snagged.

Tommy by this time was looking very pensive and furtively glancing at his watch as time was marching on. At last he produced from his pocket a long length of rolled tobacco like a thick bootlace, called Bogey Roll or Black Twist, and said with a wry smile, "I'll shift the b——or we will be here all night." With that he cut off some three inches of the tobacco and folded it into a loop, then bade me lower my line so that he could catch it in his hand. He then looped the length of tobacco round my line and tied the two ends together with a piece of string. He then let it run down my line and told me to exert pressure so as to keep the line tight. I was not only amused but amazed at this performance, whereupon I was sternly told to watch out as the fish would take off. The words were no sooner out of his mouth when the fish shot off and roared round the pool, leaping in the air as it did so. Luckily however, it did not leave the pool.

A few minutes later a shining bar of silver lay at our feet having been deftly gaffed under the chin by Tommy, who said with a beaming smile, "That fixed the crafty devil, didn't it?" The fish weighed 29.3.4 lbs, not quite 30 lb, but to me it was worth its weight in gold.

Tommy told me afterwards that it was an old trick told to him by his father years ago, which he himself had only used once before with great success. The theory was that the plug of tobacco runs down the line and lodges at the fly, and the juice of the tobacco is then sucked into the fish's mouth as it breathes and irritates the gill mechanism. Whether this is actually fact or fiction, there is certainly no doubt that it worked extremely well on that occasion.

I dread to think how long I would have been playing that fish if Tommy had not conjured up his father's trick. As it happened we did manage to return to the Home Pool for a quarter of an hour, but it was time well spent as I caught an 8 lb fish covered in sea lice before the light went.

So ended yet another delightful day on the river and as usual, I learnt yet another interesting tip from one of nature's gentlemen.

Neil Graesser

FISHING FOR ALLIGATORS

I am perhaps one of the very few men who have fished successfully for alligators, and I have caught only seven. One of the largest (measuring 18ft in and in girth 11ft 3in) ran out 30 fathoms of 1½inch white Manilla rope, and then dragged 27 men, the odd seven of whom were Europeans, up to their waists in mud and water, only giving in when choked by his mouth being kept open by the way in which he was hooked. The head of this alligator is now in my possession, and weighs 63lb.

Your correspondent's sketches and theories may catch the unwary sportsman, but I question whether they will ever catch an alligator. I studied how to catch them in the Hoohly for years, and the only bait I ever found they would look at was the lights and lungs of a pig left with about three or four inches of windpipe attached, through which the bait was inflated, and so floated. The hook or hooks used were shark hooks, but not of the ordinary shark make. They must be fine steel, and very thick in the bend; ordinary shark hooks will straighten. I have one now, which did not catch, straightened, and even had the barb torn away.

Add to this, there is, as far as I know, but one place where an alligator can be hooked securely, and that is at the back of the roof of the mouth. When the hook fixed there, and there only, were they landed. Two hooks should be used, wired back to back, and the greatest possible care taken to conceal the hooks, for the beasts are as wily as foxes.

I write these few lines as a warning. No fishing in the world requires more patience. It will take six months to catch as many, and when hooked, beware! They are the most powerful brutes in the water I ever tackled, and would walk away with and smash a fleet of boats, hoisting tackle and all, before you could say "Jack Robinson".

Nothing under white Manilla, and that 1½inch, will hold them, and an ordinary shark hook will not. Shooting is of no use in the water.

"An Old Indian", 1869

CATCH AND RELEASE

O.S. Hintz was Editor of the New Zealand Herald. His classic book of stories from the Lake Taupo region includes several memorable encounters between democratic local anglers and privileged visitors. Fred Fletcher was one of Hintz's favourite Taupo characters.

There were two American tourists living opulently somewhere in Taupo and visiting Waitahanui daily more to brag about their own skill and the extreme costliness of their gear than to fish. They were the Americans of pre-war English musical comedy, loud-voiced, harsh and arrogant – a type mercifully rare in real life. After a couple of days Fred loathed the sight of them.

We were standing on the Lodge verandah one morning when the Americans arrived in their glossy hired car and started assembling gear at the roadside. Fred muttered some most horrible oaths, seized his huge Hardy "Murdoch" from the rod rack on the verandah and strode across the road down through the lupins to the Boat Pool. It must have been on his very first cast that he hooked a fish. He probably knew exactly where the fish was lying. Fred knows a lot about fish.

At the first screech of the reel the Americans abandoned their preparations and went crashing down through the lupins to see what was happening. Fred leaned back on his massive rod, winched the astonished fish in without giving it an inch of line, beached it, tugged the fly out of its jaw, put his boot under its gleaming 8-lb bulk and propelled it back into the water.

"Jeez," protested one of the Americans. "What in Pete's name did you do that for?"

"Oh," said Fred, looking up as if he had noticed them for the first time, "we always put those little b———s back here."

from *Trout at Taupo*
by O.S. Hintz, 1955.

FINAL RECKONING

My Gaff

J.C. Mottram wrote one of the most original and brilliant books about fishing ever published: Fly-fishing; Some new Arts and Mysteries (1915). His last book Thoughts on Angling was also his last word, since he died in 1945, the year of publication.

I do not write about the gaff, but of some notches upon it, made during a lifetime whenever I was lucky enough to catch fish of unusually large size. All the fish were taken by fly fishing, and they are here recorded to show what a keen fly fisherman was likely to take during about forty years, 1905–1945.

During the previous generation the fly fisherman probably had opportunities a little more favourable, although transport was not quite so easy nor rapid; in the coming generation air transport will give the wealthy fly fisherman command of the best fishing over great distances, his hunting-ground will be greatly expanded and his prospects greatly increased. One foresees long weekends in Finland after the great grayling there, or in Sweden after huge sea trout.

The first notch in the gaff records a trout. There are no notches for grayling because one larger than 2½ lb was never caught, and I had set myself 3 lb as the lowest limit worthy of record. Many years ago, on the Kennet at grannom time, I caught a great grayling which must have weighed close upon 4 lb; it was from a

209

Society's water and, according to their rules, out of season – I put it back regretfully. I hooked and played one above 3 lb in August, at the bottom end of the marsh at Hungerford. There was a fall of red ants; hurriedly I tied one by the waterside, and with it rose and hooked the monster. I played it fearfully and very lightly; this was a mistake, because grayling when not quickly landed are liable to gain a second wind and rush wildly about, even jumping out of the water. This one did and so broke away.

The first notch is at 19 inches, for a trout of 5 lb 2 oz. I have caught four trout over 5 lb on the Kennet, but this one was not on May-fly but an olive nymph on 4X gut. I had been fishing the Lambourne during the morning and was walking down the canal after tea to fish the Kennet at Thatcham when I saw a great trout swimming slowly up the canal near the surface. I hurriedly released the nymph and switched out some line and, bending down as the fish came opposite me, I cast out the nymph and drew it across its nose. The trout turned and followed it, slowly opened its great mouth and swallowed it; I waited until the fish had turned back before tightening. The fish was not very perturbed, allowing me to walk quickly beside it, guiding the cast now on one side, now on the other of the many weed beds which were passed. The fish was not scared by my presence on the bank, probaby because it was used to pedestrians. Presently the fish turned round and we walked down a long way, then we again walked up, arriving close to where it was hooked. By this time signs of fatigue were apparent, so choosing a place clear of weeds, I held the fish firmly, played it out and landed it. I did not really enjoy playing that fish, all the time fearing the 4X gut.

The next notch is at 20 inches, for a Kennet trout of 6 lb and one-sixteenth of an ounce, on a Mayfly.

The third notch, at 21½ inches, represents a trout of 6¼ lb caught from Butcombe Bay, on Blagdon, on a no. 1 Wickham fished dry on a calm evening, when many trout were rising. This fish made one long sustained run, straight down into the abysmal depths of the reservoir; in spite of hard braking he went on and on until 30 yards of line and 70 to 80 yards of backing were out. I began to be very fearful that he would take my all, but at long last he slowed up and stopped; then I was allowed to reel him in with hardly a struggle, though a long job. After he was on a short line he made a few circles round me, then came quietly into the net: a curious battle. The fish was the record Blagdon trout for that year.

Beyond this notch and before coming to those for sea trout, there could have been notches for large brown and rainbow trout in New Zealand, but I was there at the peak of big fish, when trout in their teens were of no particular account.

The next notch, at 30 inches, represents a 12¾ lb sea trout taken from the River Dovey; it was caught on the last day of a holiday. I was fishing for salmon and thought it was one, but after reaching home I took some scales and was astounded, on looking down the microscope, to see that it was a sea trout about nine years old, which had spawned five times. It was the second fly-caught sea trout for the British Isles of the year.

A second sea trout notch is at 31 inches, the weight 14 lb. An account of the great battle this Norwegian fish fought is given elsewhere.

The salmon notches begin with a little fish of 32 lb at 42½ inches; it was my first 30-pounder, and for the River Stordal a big fish.

The next was at 43 inches, weighing 35 lb. I recorded her because, in killing her, she nearly killed me: she died on the River Eira. The upper beat of this short river between River Eira and the sea, when the snow first melts, is a terrifying sight of tumbling, spouting, roaring white water. Until the water falls not many fish reach the upper beat. The going is too bad for ascending fish; he would be in for a very rough time. After fishing two days blank, this fish was hooked on a large fly on very thick gut, in a small flat close inshore. I tried to hold him there, but steadily lost ground, and, when it became obvious that he must go down, I yelled for the boat. A little distance below was a wooden trestle bridge with trestles only about ten yards apart. The boat had to shoot these and care taken to choose the arch which the fish would be most likely to use; it seemed doubtful which of two the fish would make for, so I gave a tremendous heave to pull him over to the arch more favourable to us. Then I had to let everything go whilst I kept the point of the rod down to avoid the bridge. We shot through, boiling water tossing the boat about alarmingly. The gillie quickly put out the oars, which had been shipped, and I lifted the rod, finding the fish still with us below the bridge. We edged shoreward and about 200 yards down went ashore, where there was a little slack water; there I had to hold the fish with the rod pointing almost directly at him, but step by step I lost ground, and when the fish sidled off into white water I had again hurriedly to enter the boat which the gillie had kept handy. Over a distance of three miles we did this six times. Only occasionally could I walk the fish a few yards up-stream, quickly to lose this advantage as soon as ever the fish willed it. During the passage downstream we had to pass through some dreadful places of rocks and spouting waters, where, in cold blood, I would have been paralysed with fear. We now came to the site of an old fish-trap, where a number of piles and stakes protruded from the angry water; among these was only one small gap where the trap itself was located; the piles were the remains of a pallisade directing the fish into the trap. The gillie told me to reel in the salmon close to the boat, for by this time the fish was very tired and little more than a dead weight in the water. Shooting this gap was a clever feat of water-lore and boatmanship; there was no room for error, or rather the speed gave no time for any error to be corrected. It was a place where some years previously there had been a total wreck; happily I did not know this at the time. Having shot the gap, we entered an enormous whirlpool lying behind the piles which had diverted most of the river to the far side. Here I went ashore and for the first time gained control over the fish, which was carried round and round the whirl of water; whenever it passed near the main current I pulled hard to keep it out of this, and whenever it came near the shore I pulled hard to try to bring it to gaff. After three or four times round the pool it came to the top. The first sight of the fish was a disappointment: I had hoped for a 50-pounder – a by no means uncommon size for the Eira, but it was not in this class. The next time round brought the fish just within reach of a long gaff and the fight ended.

After a long rest I went to look at the fish; the gillie had carried her far inland. She was a brilliant block of silver, gracefully streamlined, but with a huge wound in the side of her face so large that I could put my hand through it. The gillie told me that nearly all the big fish hooked when the river was at its full height were lost through the hook tearing out – sometimes a piece of flesh is found impaled on the fly; he also said that he had taken out anglers too timid to pull hard, with the result that they were carried down another four miles to the sea.

The next notch is at 48 inches, for a 42 lb fish. Apart from knowing that this was my first 40-pounder, I can remember nothing about it; evidently it was an uneventful capture.

The last notch records my largest salmon, 45 lb, at 56 inches. It was on Sand River. The gillie and I had finished lunch, so I asked him to make a fire and brew some coffee whilst I walked down to a small pool beyond a little pine wood. I fished it down with a three-quarter inch Thunder, killed a 15-pounder halfway down and had made the very last cast at the bottom when bang! she went. The fish went right across to the far side and kept there, 80 yards away, for a long time coursing up and down. All I could do was to hold the rod above my head to prevent drowned line. After working up a long way, she started across and I was able to pull her over to my side; then she backed down and looked like going into a backwater below, full of water-logged trees, so I had to keep walking her up. She refrained from gymnastics, but seemed stubborn and heavy; at last I had a sight of her and was astounded at her great size. It seemed possible that she was a 50-pounder, and I had no gaff and the edge sloped too quickly for beaching, the gillie was beyond call – he had fallen asleep. She had to be tailed. Dozens of times I drew her nose to the edge and, sneaking up behind, tried to grab her tail: she was out in the river again. At last, stepping into the water, I was able to grab her tail with my right hand. Of course she struggled, and I felt I could not hold her with one hand, so I threw the rod on the shore and grabbed with both hands. She then gave a violent flop which knocked me off my feet and, having no hands, I went full length into the water. The salmon and I drifted down in a sort of rough-and-tumble fight, the salmon struggling to be free, I to regain my feet; thus we drifted down about twenty yards, getting into water up to my middle, but at last I regained my feet and carried my fish a long way inland: connection with the rod had long since been severed. When I waked the gillie and told him of the two fish without a gaff, one a 50-pounder, he would not believe me. He was right; it was 5 pounds short of every angler's wish.

from *Thoughts on Angling*
by J.C. Mottram, 1945

SOURCES

"The Battle of Bolstadoyri" by Terry Golding from *Trout & Salmon*.

"An Early Start" by W. Bromley-Davenport from *Sport*, 1885.

"Landing the Record Tay Salmon" by Georgina Ballantine from *The Fishing Gazette*.

"An Excursion with the March Brown" by Patrick R. Chalmers from *At the Tail of the Weir*, 1932.

"Mr Thornton's 50-pounders" by H. G. Thornton from *Salmon & Trout*.

"By the Skin of his Teeth" from *Days & Nights of Salmon Fishing* by William Scrope, 1843.

"No Flies on Jim" from *The Man-Eating Leopard of Rudraprayag* by Jim Corbett, O.U.P.

"Dinner in the Field" by "K" from *The Field*, 1869.

"How to Catch a Crocodile", "Occasional Hazards" and "Big Fish Reel" from *The Rod in India* by H. S. Thomas, 3rd ed. 1897.

"The Fish of My Dreams" from *The Man-Eater of Kumaon* by Jim Corbett, O.U.P.

"At the Mouth of the Klamath" from *Tales of Fresh-Water Fishing* by Zane Grey, 1928.

"The Sulking Salmon" from *Fish Facts and Fancies* by F. Gray Griswold, 1923.

"Three Weeks Later" from *Salmon–Fishing on the Grand Cascapedia* by Edmund W. Davis, 1904.

"The Nore" from *Fishing: Fact or Fantasy?* by G. D. Luard, Faber & Faber, 1947.

"A Good Day on the Shannon" from *The Practice of Angling particularly as regards Ireland* by O'Gorman, 1845.

"In the Money" from *Fisherman* by Anthony Pearson, Pelham Books.

"Good Neighbours" from *A Man May Fish* by T. C. Kingsmill Moore, 2nd ed. Colin Smythe Ltd, 1979.

"The Record Spring Salmon" by Doreen Davey from *The Fishing Gazette*.

"A Fighting Usk Salmon" from *The Field*.

"Big Fish" from *Tales of a Wye Fisherman* by H. A. Gilbert.

"Tale of an Unsung Salmon" by Tony Gubba from *Trout & Salmon*.

"Big Fish River" from *A Salmon–Fisher's Odyssey* by John Ashley-Cooper, H. F. & G. Witherby, 1982.

"Big Fish Fly" from *Techniques of Trout fishing and Fly Tying* by George Harvey, Revised ed. Lyons & Burford NY.

"Float Fishing in South Africa" from *Game Fish Records* by "Jock Scott", H. F. & G. Witherby, 1936.

"The Anniversary" by D. C. Dinesen from *Jaeger & Fisker*, Copenhagen.

"It Came as a Big Surprise" by Byron Rogers from *The Sunday Telegraph*.

"Tricks of the Trade" from *Big Trout* by William H. Lawrie, Oliver & Boyd, 1955.

"Fishing for Alligators" from *The Field*.

"Catch and Release" from *Trout at Taupo* by O. S. Hintz, Max Reinhardt, 1955.

"My Gaff" from *Thoughts on Angling* by J. C. Mottram, Herbert Jenkins, 1945.

ACKNOWLEDGMENTS

The Editors acknowledge with heartfelt gratitude the contri-
butions of those authors who provided material especially
for   this book:

Dr J. R. Holden
Lilla Rowcliffe
Ian Niall
Alison Faulkner
Richard Waddington
Neil Graesser
Douglas Pilkington
Odd Haraldsen

Further grateful acknowledgment is due to those who kindly
provided photographs from private collections.